WINNING WITH OPTIONS TRADING

FROM THE BASICS TO LEVERAGING THE BEST STRATEGIES FOR EXPLOSIVE INCOME—A STRAIGHTFORWARD CRASH COURSE FOR BEGINNERS

WINNING FINANCE PUBLICATIONS

© **Copyright 2022 - All rights reserved.**

The content contained within this book may not be reproduced, duplicated, or transmitted without direct written permission from the author or the publisher.

Under no circumstances will any blame or legal responsibility be held against the publisher, or author, for any damages, reparation, or monetary loss due to the information contained within this book, either directly or indirectly.

Legal Notice:

This book is copyright protected. It is only for personal use. You cannot amend, distribute, sell, use, quote, or paraphrase any part, or the content within this book, without the consent of the author or publisher.

Disclaimer Notice:

Please note the information contained within this document is for educational and entertainment purposes only. All effort has been executed to present accurate, up-to-date, reliable, and complete information. No warranties of any kind are declared or implied. Readers acknowledge that the author is not engaged in the rendering of legal, financial, medical, or professional advice. The content within this book has been derived from various sources. Please consult a licensed professional before attempting any techniques outlined in this book.

By reading this document, the reader agrees that under no circumstances is the author responsible for any direct or indirect losses incurred as a result of the use of the information contained within this document, including, but not limited to, errors, omissions, or inaccuracies.

CONTENTS

Introduction   5

1. WHAT ARE OPTIONS?   7
   Future Contracts   8
   Options Contract   8
   Types of Option Contracts   9
   Other Important Terminology   17

2. THE BENEFITS AND RISKS OF OPTIONS   21
   Reasons to Trade with Options   21
   The Risks   25

3. EXERCISE, ASSIGNMENT, AND CLOSING TRADES   31
   Closing the Position   33
   Exercising and Assignment Expanded   36

4. PRICING   41
   How Do Premiums Work?   42
   Time Value and Time Decay   44
   Implied Volatility   46

5. THE GREEKS AND THEIR RELEVANCE TO THE PRICE   55
   Delta   55
   Gamma   58
   Theta   59
   Vega   60
   Minor Greeks   61

6. THE GENERAL RULES OF A GOOD TRADER   65
   The Psychology of Investing and Its Importance   65
   Setting the Rules   68
   Risk Management   68

Logging Your Trades	73
Backtesting	75
Paper Trading	75
Characteristics of a Winning Trader	76
Habits of a Winning Trader	79
Technical Analysis With Options	80
Technical Indicators for Options Trading	86
Fundamental Analysis With Option Trading	90
Understanding Ticker Symbols	92

7. GETTING THE MOST OUT OF OPTIONS
   CONTRACTS 95
   Index and ETF Options 95
   Getting Started 96
   Basic Strategies When Buying Calls and Puts 100

8. ADVANCED STRATEGIES 113
   Neutral Strategies 114
   Bullish Strategies 140
   Bearish Strategies 149
   LEAPS 153
   Other Considerations 154
   When to Sell? 155
   Trailing Stop 156
   Partial Profit Booking 157

   Conclusion 159
   References 161

INTRODUCTION

Options sometimes have the wrong connotations. Most investors believe they are complicated and will lead to a loss of a lot of money for them. That's simply not true. Hopefully, you'll understand why once you read this book. Trading stocks in the market can lead to good profits. However, adding options to one's arsenal gives the investor many more tactics that should ultimately end with him receiving higher returns with only a fraction of the capital spent. Of course, risks are involved, but in this book, you'll learn about the basics of options and how to mitigate most of the risks involved with trading options. With this book, you'll have a comprehensive guide that starts with the basics of what options are and covers everything until, eventually, the reader will be comfortable utilizing advanced strategies to make money. Everything is written in a simple manner, so the book is suitable for beginners and more experienced traders alike. You'll have a detailed explanation of every term, so you don't have to worry about the jargon you sometimes stumble upon when trying to read about options.

As previously stated, we begin with the fundamentals of options: what exactly they are, their characteristics, and their various styles of use. We also focus on indicators that help assess the risks and rewards of a particular option strategy. We also have a dedicated chapter on general rules that will make you a great trader. There's a lot more information, but it's all thoroughly detailed, so you can easily understand everything.

Most importantly, this is a very comprehensive and detailed book, written while having in mind the type of person who doesn't know about options at all but wants to learn more and be able to start their own trades.

Winning Finance Publications is a group of investors who've studied and had real experience with the market for many years. Our mission is to help people be in control of their financial future. We do this by making accessible as much information as possible in an easy-to-understand way while putting an emphasis on giving the information over in a practical way so that the reader can actually use the information to make money.

In sum, we want you to be a successful investor, and with the information in this book, you can be one!

1

WHAT ARE OPTIONS?

In their most basic definition, an options contract is a written agreement between two parties regarding another asset (e.g., shares of a company). This agreement states that concerning this asset, one party has the right to enforce a specific transaction from the other - specifically, the right to enforce the buying or selling of the asset, depending on the contract. These contracts include relevant details such as whether it is a right to buy or a right to sell, how long this right lasts, and the price at which the transaction can be carried out. To understand this concept better, let's look at two different types of contracts first: futures contracts and options contracts.

FUTURE CONTRACTS

These are contracts agreed upon between two parties (a buyer and a seller) in which one participant agrees to buy a specific asset for a specific price at a specific time in the future. For example, suppose an investor purchases a futures contract entitling him to 100 barrels of gasoline for a given price at a specific date in the future. In this case, he must buy the barrels of gasoline when the agreed date arrives, even if the price has dropped in the interim. Just like the buyer of the contract, the seller of the contract must also accept to sell the barrels at the agreed-upon date for the agreed-upon amount even if, in the meantime, the price of gasoline has risen.

OPTIONS CONTRACT

While options share almost all the same characteristics with futures, as discussed further below, there is an essential difference between them. With a futures contract, the two parties involved must satisfy the terms of the agreement and therefore make the transaction according to the agreed-upon conditions. With an options contract, however, the contract gives the purchaser the right to enforce the contract but not the obligation - hence the term "option."

Therefore when comparing ordinary options contracts with futures contracts, with options contracts, the buyer has the right but not the obligation to activate the contract. In contrast, with futures, the buyer and the seller have an obligation to fulfill the contract.

In all other respects, an options contract is the same as a futures contract. The details of the price, date, and asset are all contained within the contract and set at the time of the agreement. These will all be elaborated on later in the book.

Like futures, options are financial instruments that are derivatives. This means that their price is linked to an underlying asset, which means that their price is intrinsically connected to whatever happens to the asset they represent. Hence the name derivative - their price is derived from another asset's value. A typical example of an underlying asset is stocks. In fact, in this book, we will interchange the terms "underlying asset" and "underlying stock" since stocks are the most common type of underlying asset.

TYPES OF OPTION CONTRACTS

There are two types of options: a call option and a put option. A call option is when the contract purchaser has the right to buy the underlying asset specified in the contract from the seller of the contract - also known as the writer of the contract. A put option is when the contract purchaser has the right to sell the underlying asset to the contract writer. Simply put, buying a call option gives you the right to purchase a certain security, while buying a put option gives you the right to sell it.

When we refer to call options, one concept you will often hear is a "long call." This is when you buy the call option as opposed to selling/writing it, which would be a "short call." The terms long and short are used very often in the investing world. The term "long" refers to when the investor wants to hold the asset, for example, in this case, when the purchaser of the option contract intends to have the contract (therefore, he is "long the call"). In contrast, the term "short" is when the investor doesn't want to hold the asset, for example, the option writer who doesn't want to keep the contract - instead, he wants to sell it to someone else (therefore he is "short the call").

With call options, if the underlying asset rises, so will the price of the call. Option calls don't have a limit on how high their price can reach; since their price is tied to the underlying asset and the price of the underlying asset can increase indefinitely, the price of the contract also has no upper limit. However, the maximum an investor can lose if the price doesn't go up is the price paid for the option. This price is called the "option premium." Let's have a look at an illustrative example.

If you are a potential homebuyer with the chance to purchase a call option from a developer, let's look at how this could look. You are given the opportunity to buy a contract that gives you the right to buy a house for $300,000 at any time in the next two years. In this case, $300,000 is the agreed-upon amount and is referred to as the "strike price."

The two-year limit is the time period you have to activate this right, and the date two years from now is referred to as the "expiry date." The developer would demand you pay him for this right. This is the premium. In this example, let's say the premium to purchase the call option was 10% of the price of the house at the moment, or $30,000. Like all call option premiums, this money is non-refundable.

Imagine that after a year, the developer has upgraded the area, and there are many more amenities around, as well as more buildings, and the house is valued at $600,000. Because your option contract gives you the right to purchase the property for $300,000, you can now activate this right and buy the house for $300,000 below market price (giving you a profit of $300,000). However, should the opposite happen, and the area has some issues that cause the property to decrease in price, although you will decide not to activate your right to purchase the property (since its market value is less than $300,000), the initial $30,000 collected doesn't come back to you. This example helps to identify the key characteristics of an options contract, such as the strike price, expiry date, and premium. It also helps illuminate the profit potential and risk profile, which is always vital to know before entering a trade. Specifically, it becomes clear why the profit potential is unlimited, i.e., the investor paid a fixed $30,000 for the right, yet the property's value can rise endlessly (in this case, it doubled).

In contrast, the losses are restricted because the investor's sole investment is the premium paid, or $30,000. We can therefore say that the breakeven point (the price at which there is no loss or gain) is at the strike price ($300,000) plus the premium (which was $30,000); at this point ($330,000), the value the options contract has gained is enough to offshoot the amount he paid for the contract at the beginning. Similarly, the profit will always be the amount the underlying is now ($600,000) minus the original price ($300,000) minus the premium paid (£30,000), which in this case is $270,000. The truth is that in making this calculation, it is important to minus other costs too, such as the commissions paid to the brokers, etc. however, since these costs vary from case to case, and in the case of stock options, they are often zero, for the sake of simplicity we will ignore these costs and generally assume there are none.

We will go more in-depth on what constitutes the premium, but for now, it is enough to realize that it is simply the price of the option in the current market.

A put option is the inverse of a call option in that it grants the investor the right to sell the underlying security at the strike price. When the underlying asset loses value, the put option gains it. It is important to realize that you don't need to own the asset that you are buying the put on. For example, if a stock is currently trading at $500 and you purchase a put option for $4 that allows you to sell it at $450 (this is the strike price), if the stock goes down to $350, you would be able to buy the shares at $350 and then resell them for $450 to the person who sold you the option contract. This means you will have a $100 gain minus the $4 you paid for this right, a total of $96.

If we look at the risk-reward profile of a put option, we can see that the maximum you can lose is the same as buying a call, namely the premium you paid for the option, in this case, $4. However, the reward profile is different here. Since your gain is decided by how much the underlying decreases below the strike price, the profit is capped by how much the price can indeed drop. In this case, since the strike price is $450, the most the price can drop is $450. This means that the maximum you can earn from this contract, and put contracts in general, is the strike price ($450) minus the premium paid ($4), which is a total of $446. The breakeven point will be when the underlying asset is at the strike price ($450) minus the premium ($4) since, at this point ($446), the gain you have made from the option's value will offshoot what you paid for the option, i.e., the premium.

We have now discussed two possible trades, buying a call option and buying a put option. When taking one of these two positions, you are on the buy side of the transaction; however, there are another two possibilities when trading options contracts, i.e., selling the call option and selling the put option. The more technical term for selling a contract is writing a contract. When writing an options contract, you are selling to someone else the right to enforce a transaction with you. In the case of writing a call, you are selling to the other party the right to buy the underlying asset from you, and in the case of a put option, you are selling to the other party the right to sell you the underlying asset.

Once again, it is of value to point out that one can write a call on a stock even if he doesn't own it. He just needs to commit to buying the stock if necessary, i.e., when the purchaser of the call option enforces the contract.

When you are writing options, your payout is entirely different from when you are buying options. You make a profit straight away in the form of the options premium that you collect; this is the maximum profit you can make, and your plan is to retain as much of this as possible.

The risk-reward profile is the opposite of what it is when buying options. When writing options, the profits are capped to the amount of the premium, not the losses. The amount you can lose mirrors what we wrote above regarding the amount you can gain by being the purchaser of the option. In the case of writing a call, your loss potential is unlimited as the price of the underlying can go up indefinitely. Being the contract writer means you are obligated to sell the underlying for the agreed-upon price no matter how much the underlying costs now. In the case of writing a put option, your loss potential is large but not unlimited. The maximum loss is the amount the underlying can lose minus the premium you have already taken as profit. This is because you need to buy the underlying at the agreed-upon price even if the current market price is $0.

The breakeven points when selling options will be the same as the breakeven points when buying options. The seller of a call is at breakeven when the stock price is above the strike price by the amount he received as the premium; this is because, at this point, the loss from the contract cancels out the gain from collecting the premium. In the case of writing a put, it is the same. When the stock price is below the strike price by the amount he received as the premium, this will also be the breakeven point because the loss from the contract will cancel out the initial profit from collecting the premium.

As an options trader, this gives you four possible positions: buying a call option, selling a call option, buying a put option, or selling a put option.

Whatever option you choose, you will always be speculating on the price of an underlying asset.

To recap, when it comes to call options, the buyer of the call is speculating that the price will go above the strike price by more than the amount he paid as the premium; otherwise, he still makes a loss. The seller doesn't expect it to go above the strike price, and he starts to make a loss when the underlying gains enough that it also surpasses the amount he got for the premium.

With put options, the buyer speculates that the market price of an underlying security will decrease and fall below the strike price by more than the amount he paid as the premium, while the seller of a put option speculates that the price won't fall beyond the strike price.

Both buyers of puts and calls have limited losses—the premium paid for the option. On the other hand, sellers of options can lose a lot more. The seller of a call option can have unlimited losses in theory, while the maximum loss of a seller of a put option is equal to the strike price minus the premium he received from the option buyer.

These are the only four possible trades that an options trader can make, and therefore they form the foundation of all option trading techniques and strategies.

In order to make these trades in your brokerage account, there are two important terms that you need to know. These are "to open" and "to close." The term "to open" refers to opening a position by creating a contract, and "to close" refers to closing the options already open. This practically means that when trying to buy options, when wanting to buy a call or put, you place a "buy to open" order (how to know whether it is a call or put and other details on practically placing orders are explained later on). When you want to write/sell a call or put, you use the "sell to open" when placing the order.

[If you "buy to open," you'd be taking a long position because you are expecting the contract to go up in value, while with a "sell to open," you'd be taking a short position because you are expecting the contract to decrease in value.]

"Buy to close" and "Sell to close" are used to close these open trades.

So if you opened a position with a "buy to open," you can close it with a "sell to close" order, while if you opened with a "sell to open," you can close the position with a "buy to close" order. We will take a deeper look at closing positions in chapter 3.

OTHER IMPORTANT TERMINOLOGY

We've mentioned certain terms, such as "strike price" and "expiration date," throughout the chapter. While some of these can be easily understood in their context, let's go through some of the most common terms and clearly explain them.

Strike Price, ITM, OTM, and ATM

The strike price of an option is the price agreed to in the contract at which the underlying asset can be bought or sold once the contract is exercised. For call options, the strike price is the value at which the option holder can buy the underlying asset; for put options, the strike price refers to the price at which the option holder can sell the underlying asset. The strike price is created when writing the contract. To the investor, this information tells them the price the underlying security has to attain before the contract starts to make money. The technical term for this is "In the money" (ITM). ITM means (in the case of a call) that the market price (e.g., $60) is higher than the strike price (e.g., $50). If the contract indeed expires with this market value for the underlying asset, the difference between this price and the strike price (e.g., $10) is the profit the holder can earn by activating his contract since he can now buy a $60 stock for $50. In this example, we would say that this contract is "$10 in the money".

If the underlying asset's market price (e.g., $40) is below the strike price, then the call option is "Out of the money" (OTM), and there is no profit for the contract holder to make, in this case, we say the option is "$10 out the money".

There is also the concept of "At the money" (ATM), which refers to when the market price is the same as the strike price. At this point, too, there is yet to be a profit for the contract holder; however, there is still a good chance of it because the underlying price is very near to making the option profitable. This term is used loosely to refer to any price near the strike price (e.g., $49 & $51).

Regarding put options, ITM and OTM are the reverse. When the market price is below the strike price, it is "In the money" because, at this point, it is in the profit zone (i.e., the investor can buy it for the market value and force the option writer to buy it for the higher agreed upon price). It is "Out the money" if the underlying price is above the strike price since, at this point, it is out of the profit zone.

Expiration Date

The expiration date of an options contract is the last day of the contract. This means that the contracts are no longer valid after the expiration date. Investors can choose to exercise the contract at any time before this date, but if they let it expire, it becomes worthless.

The "expiration date" will always be given as a month; however, its exact date will vary according to the derivative the investor holds. If you hold a contract for a listed stock option in the U.S., the expiration date is usually the third Friday of the month that the contract expires. If this falls on a holiday, then the expiration date is moved to the Thursday before. Investors and traders must decide what to do with their options or futures contracts before the expiration date, or their contract becomes worthless.

However, some contracts have what is called an "automatic exercise provision" that automatically exercises options that are ITM by the expiration date.

Options Premium

The current market price of an option contract is called an "option premium." In other words, this is the price a buyer and seller agree on when trading a contract. This price is (generally) continuously changing, just like prices for shares continually change. This is because, for any set of specifications (i.e., expiry date, strike price, etc.), there will be many options contracts with these specifications. Additionally, option contracts can be resold like shares, since the option holder can sell his right to someone else. This leads to many sales happening, leading to a constantly changing price.

With stock options, the premium is shown as an amount per share, although most contracts are for 100 shares. For example, if the price shown in your account is $3, then this means that you will pay $300 because it's the premium times the 100 shares.

Option writers sell options and, as a reward, get the option premium as income. An option premium is composed of intrinsic and extrinsic values and will be explained later.

In this chapter, we've focused on what options are, how they work, and their basic types. In the following chapter, we'll discuss the benefits and risks involved with trading options.

2

THE BENEFITS AND RISKS OF OPTIONS

There are certainly benefits to purchasing options; however, there are also risks that you must consider.

REASONS TO TRADE WITH OPTIONS

Although investing in options can be deemed riskier than stock investments, these perceived risks can be reduced and controlled once one understands them. In fact, in some instances, by using the appropriate approach, one can almost entirely eliminate the risk. Let's first take a look at the advantages options provide.

Cost-Efficient

Options are often cost-efficient alternatives because they tend to have good leveraging power. In other words, an options trader can have an identical position in terms of how much stock they control, but for a fraction of the cost. For example, say you want to control 100 shares of a $100 stock; you can purchase one call contract (which controls 100 shares) with a strike price of $100. Assuming the premium of the option is about 10% of the share price, this call option would cost you about $1000 ($10 x 100 shares). If, on the other hand, you bought the shares outright, you would have had to lay out the entire $10,000. By using a call option, you now have an extra $9000 that isn't tied to this investment.

What is important here is that you don't lose out on any profits by owning the options as opposed to the actual shares. Imagine the price of the underlying rises to $105. If you hold the shares themselves, your original $10,000 has now risen to $10,500, which is a profit of $500. If you own the call option, this, in theory, allows you to buy the shares for $10,000 and sell them for $10,500, also giving you the same profit. However, what is neat here is that, as explained later, an options trader will rarely activate his contract; instead, the entire profit - in this case, $500 - will be added to the premium of the options themselves. This means you can bag this $500 profit by simply selling the options for their current value without needing to activate them and then go and buy and sell the shares. In practice, you have made the same profit by simply buying and then selling the call option. In fact, very often, when buying and selling the actual shares, the commissions will be very significant because you are trading with 1000 shares, whereas if using options, you are dealing with one option contract and hence have a smaller commission.

Less Risky

If used carefully, options are, in fact, less risky than stock investments. In other words, there are times when trading options can significantly reduce the risk of investing. This is true because traders require less money to control shares when using options. For example, imagine you buy a call option with a strike price of $60 on a stock currently trading at $65 for a premium of $7. If the stock price drops from $65 to $50 and your option becomes worthless, you have only lost the $7 you paid for the premium. If you had been holding the stock, you would have lost $15 on every share.

Higher Potential Returns

Options often have a higher potential return. This is simple to understand because, as explained earlier, you put up less money when using options, yet you make the same profit in dollar terms. If you pay less for an investment, you will have a higher return percentage. In our example earlier on, when you buy a call contract for $1000, and you make a $500 profit, you have made a 50% return on your original capital, as opposed to holding the actual shares where your $10,000 makes a $500 profit which is only a 5% gain. Another way of thinking about it is to imagine you also invested $10,000 into the options (by buying ten calls). In this case, the profit would be $5000 (50%) instead of $500.

Obviously, this only happens if your assumption regarding the price movement is correct.

Flexibility

Lastly, options allow for more flexibility than equity. This is because they present many alternatives that can mimic other positions. These are often called synthetic positions, enabling the investor to style his trade to gain in many new ways.

For example, they make it possible for the investor to make gains from different phenomena, e.g., unlike traditional stock trading, the investor can make money using options even when the stock price is not moving in any direction. This is because, as we'll see later, besides price direction, other factors also influence the price of an options contract, such as the time before expiration and the amount of expected volatility. This lets the investor profit by being correct in his predictions of these two parameters, even when the underlying asset's price does not change.

Practically, a synthetic position does this by utilizing a mix of both puts and calls. You will better understand this once you read the chapters on options pricing and advanced strategies below.

Another example of options flexibility is that in addition to making money, options can also be used to protect your portfolio. This is called hedging and is discussed in detail in a later chapter.

THE RISKS

When it comes to options, the obvious first risk is losing the money you invested. However, these losses express themselves in two ways, depending on whether you are purchasing the options or writing/selling them. The loss in the first situation is limited to the premium price (i.e., the total you put into the investment); in the second situation, the loss can be significantly more. As a result, it is necessary to look over each option trade independently to understand each trade's risk profile.

We've talked about call holders (those that buy the calls), put holders, call writers, and put writers; all of these have different risks.

In the previous chapter, we discussed the specific risk-reward profile of all four types of positions; this is crucial since investors must always know their potential rewards, risks, and breakeven points.

Buying on Margin

One risk associated with selling options is the need for margin. When we talk about buying on margin, we often mean borrowing money to increase profits. For example, if you can invest $1,000 in a single stock and, after a year, get a 15% return, you'll make $150. Consider borrowing another $1,000 (from the broker) to buy additional stock and double your figures. You now have a 30% return on your investment. This is called buying on margin. Nothing guarantees you that you'll make a profit on the borrowed money; in fact, if the share price decreases, this will magnify your losses since besides the losses on your own $1000, you now have losses on the borrowed $1000 too. Because the brokerage will want to guarantee that it gets paid back in full even if your investment loses, it will only lend you money if you put up assets as collateral. This makes buying on margin a risky strategy since if you lose too much, the brokerage will start selling your other investments to get back their money.

When it comes to option margins, this works a little differently. An option margin is the collateral that an investor must deposit in their account in order to sell options. Since when selling options, the losses can get immense and out of control; therefore, the writer needs enough set aside to ensure he can honor the contract even in the case of large losses. If, for example, an investor wants to write a call option contract for Apple shares with a strike price of $200 however, when he writes the contract, he doesn't own the shares; when the share price goes to $210, he now needs to spend $21,000 to buy the shares (since a contract represents 100 shares) to then sell them to the option buyer. Therefore the brokerage will only allow him to sell if he has this value set aside as collateral. Now imagine the price of Apple shares keeps going up, and he has put $25,000 as collateral. If the share price were to reach $260, he wouldn't have enough money to honor his contract (since he needs $26,000 and only has $25,000). Therefore, the brokerage will not allow this to happen and will sell his collateral for $25,000 when the share price reaches $250. The risks here are very apparent; the loss of this trade can end up with him losing many other assets that were used as collateral.

These are requirements that everyone has to follow and are written by the Federal Reserve Board. As we've seen in the paragraph above, while stocks use margins to increase buying power, options use them solely as collateral. Although there's a minimum margin required, brokers can use different margins. If you are an investor and want to open a new account to utilize option margins, you must apply for trading authorization from the broker beforehand.

As previously stated, only option writers must be concerned with margin trading since purchasing calls and puts - the sorts of trades that a beginner will use - require no margin at all (because they cannot lose more than the premium they have already paid). Additionally, there are certain strategies for selling options that do not require any margin at all. The covered call strategy, which is quite common and is discussed in a later chapter, is a typical example of this.

Time Works Against You

There is one property unique to options which does indeed make them riskier than other assets. This is that when it comes to dealing with options, being right about the stock price is not enough to make you money. To make money with options, it is also essential to get your timing right. With stocks, time is on your side since the longer you wait, the more likely the price will rise and hit your target. With options, however, the opposite is true. The longer you wait, the less time there is for your contract to become profitable; therefore, time is working against you. Ultimately to profit, you need to be right about the timing just as much about the price; otherwise, the contract will expire worthless.

This risk only applies to the buyer of an option; an options seller, on the other hand, benefits from the disappearing time. This is because the seller is betting against the price hitting the strike price; therefore, as time passes, he is more likely to be correct.

This is why selling options is a far more conservative strategy than purchasing them. Time is always on the seller's side, as it is always running out for the buyer. (Though when selling, there is a potential for much bigger losses.)

Knowing the risks and benefits of dealing with options is crucial to success. When done correctly, options can be less risky than stocks, more cost-efficient, and have higher returns in a shorter time. However, there are risks too, as we've covered in this chapter.

3

EXERCISE, ASSIGNMENT, AND CLOSING TRADES

Now that we've seen one's rights and obligations once they acquire option contracts let's move on and understand how you can exit such contracts. There are various ways to do this, each with different advantages. Choosing the right one can be the difference between making a good profit and an excellent one. There are three ways to exit an options position, exercise, assignment, and closing.

"Exercising" is when the investor triggers (i.e., exercises) the right to purchase or sell the underlying stock specified in the option contract. The right to exercise an option at the strike price is only given to the option holder (buyer). The decision to do this will depend on many factors, such as the type of option, the current price of the underlying asset, the strike price, and even the length of time remaining in the contract until it reaches its expiration date. How these features affect this decision will be explained later. When an option holder exercises their option contract, they are invoking their right to purchase or sell. When this happens, the investor exchanges the options contract for the option's underlying asset at the strike price.

"Assignment" refers to the seller's obligation to fulfill the terms specified in the contract, which means they have to buy or sell depending on the option type (sell if they wrote a call and buy if they wrote a put). It is called assignment because the investor is assigned to fulfill the exercised contract of the option holder. The assignment process is totally random. If, for example, there are 1,000 traders with long call options and another 1,000 with short call options, and one of the investors with a long call decides to exercise his option, then one of the investors with a short call will be randomly assigned to exercise the notice. This is because when you sell or purchase an options contract, the party on the other side of the trade is actually the Options Clearing Corporation (OCC), who are tasked with ensuring market stability and integrity (in the U.S.); this means that the OCC is the buyer to every seller and the seller to every buyer. Therefore when an investor exercises his contract, it is arbitrary as to which short investor the OCC should assign; therefore, the OCC uses a random procedure so the process remains free from favoritism.

An obvious point that is still worth mentioning is that no investor will exercise their option unless it is indeed an in-the-money option that they will profit from through exercising.

CLOSING THE POSITION

"To close" is when a trader places a trade to exit their position, either by selling their bought option (with a "sell to close" order) at its current premium or by buying back a written/sold option (with a "buy to close" order) for its current premium. In both these cases, the loss or gain will be the difference between the premiums, the premium he received, and the premium he paid. Although one might initially think that the standard way of exiting an options contract is through exercising, this isn't the case. Instead, closing the trade is the norm when leaving an options trade, as explained below.

You will remember from earlier that there are two ways to exit through closing an order. Investors use a "sell to close" order on open long positions (calls or puts they bought), which they've used a "buy to open" order to establish in the first place. You can think of this as the trader selling the right he bought previously (i.e., the contract) to another investor. Investors use a "buy to close" order on open short positions (calls or puts they sold/wrote), which they've used a "sell to open" order to establish in the first place. (Remember, "long" refers to positions that an investor takes by holding an asset, so a long option position means he bought and now owns the contract. "Short" refers to positions that an investor takes by selling the asset, so a short option position means he sold the contract, i.e., he is the option writer). This can be thought of as the investor buying the right he previously sold back.

Using long positions as an example, the investor will "sell to close" call options when he is no longer interested in a long bullish position and "sell to close" put options when he no longer wants to hold a long bearish position.

There are three possible outcomes when you "sell to close": you "sell to close" for a profit, at breakeven, or for a loss.

Let's see how a case of closing the position for a profit could look. Say you buy a call for $7.50 (for a total of $750 once we calculate for all 100 shares represented by the call), with a strike price of $70 on a stock with a current price of $75. Let's imagine two months later, just before expiration, the stock price is at $80. Your option call will now have a premium of $10 (and total of $1000). In this case, you can sell to close the option and take the profit of $2.50 on each share (because of the $10-7.50 difference). Once again, this means you are selling the call to someone else for $10. You will be able to see that an immediate benefit of selling to close the option as opposed to exercising it, is that when closing the option, you don't need to lay out the entire $70 to buy each share to then sell the share at the market value of $80. Instead, you can sell the contract itself and get the $2.50 profit on each share. The above example illustrates how closing the trade results in the significant benefit of not needing a lot of capital at hand. There are, however, additional benefits to taking your profit by closing out of the contract. One is that it will save you in commission fees since you are saving on two significant transactions (the one to buy the shares and the one to then sell them back into the market). Another benefit is that it saves time, and yet another is that it will protect you from potential market swings that can happen between buying and selling the shares.

For the reasons just given, when exiting the position, it's usually the best move to sell to close, even when you will make the same profit from exercising. If one has additional reasons to hold the shares, e.g., he wants to hold this stock in his portfolio, then obviously exercising is the most sensible move.

There is another very significant reason to exit through closing the trade, which applies when selling for a profit before the expiry date. This reason is based on the concept of "time value," which is expanded on in the next chapter on pricing. The critical thing to know now is that before an option's expiry date, besides for the value the premium has because of the profit it can make, it has additional value from this "time value." Therefore if you "sell to close," you'd capture this time value in the premium received. However, if you exercise and your profit only comes from the actual purchase and resale of the shares, you will lose out on this extra time value which is only in the premium.

When the investor "sells to close" at breakeven, this means the price of the option's premium remains the same. When a "sell to close" happens at a loss, the option's premium is below the amount the investor bought it for; however, this doesn't mean the investor has lost everything, and therefore he can get some of the value back by selling the option on for what it is worth now.

These have all been examples of "selling to close"; however, closing through a "buy to close" will just look the opposite way around. A "buy to close" for a profit is when the investor buys back the written option for less than he sold it, thereby making a profit since the premium he originally received is more than the premium he paid now to close it. A breakeven trade will be when both premiums are the same; and "buying to close" at a loss will be when the investor needs to pay more now to close the trade than he received originally when opening it.

EXERCISING AND ASSIGNMENT EXPANDED

As we've seen, when you have the right to purchase a stock, you have a call option, and when you have the right to sell, you have a put option. When you exercise a stock option, you buy the underlying security (if it's an option call) or sell it (if it's a put option). As the option holder, you can do this any time before the expiry date. When you do this earlier, you are selling or purchasing the stock before the expiration date.

The exercising process starts when you tell your broker you want to exercise your option. There's a cutoff time that is usually one day, but this is something that you should ask your broker. If the cutoff time is one day, this means it will take one day for your option to be exercised. When exercising happens, you will acquire the underlying asset for the agreed-upon strike price. This asset could be the stock of a company or a commodity, for example.

As explained earlier, an assignment is when the seller (writer) has to either purchase or sell (depending on whether the option was a put or call) the underlying asset at the strike price. This obligation starts when the buyer exercises their right to sell or purchase the option's underlying asset. Because of this, when you sell an options contract, you can be assigned from the time you created your position until the contract expires or is closed. Being assigned is typically something the seller wants to avoid. Since it is far more desirable to close a losing position than to be assigned and need to buy all the shares (and then sell them on again in the case of a call). It can be additionally frustrating if, as the seller, you believe that in the time from now until the expiry, your position will gain in value, only to find out that you have been assigned and need to honor the contract now and take the current loss. As mentioned earlier, this risk only exists when the underlying asset is in-the-money, and the writer is in the losing position. If the option is not in-the-money, the holder will obviously not exercise it since there is no money to be made by doing so. The possibility of being assigned is therefore considered a risk to the option writer. To minimize this risk, the option writer should close his position (through a "buy to close" order) before there is a great likelihood of being assigned. To discover the likelihood of an assignment, let's first look at when it is in the best interest of the option holder to exercise his option.

We mentioned earlier that it is generally better for the holder of an option to close out of a trade rather than exercise it. This is especially the case when wanting to end the position early when there is still time value. However, there can be good reasons to exercise an option early. For example, a potential dividend is a great reason to exercise it, even early. Dividends are a distribution of earnings from a company to its shareholders. Shareholders of certain stocks get paid dividends, usually every quarter. For a shareholder to receive a dividend, they have to hold the stock by what's called the "ex-dividend date." This is a date earlier than the actual dividend date, which can legally be between two weeks and one month before the date of receiving the dividend. So, if you have a call option and want to be paid dividends from the underlying stock, you must exercise the option (sometimes earlier) in order to hold the stock by the ex-dividend date. Therefore, if the dividend to be gained is worth more than the "time value, " it is worth exercising even early to capture this gain.

Going back to the writer of an option, who has the risk of being assigned if a buyer of an option exercises it. We can sum up that assignment will be very uncommon since most option holders will want to exit through "selling to close," not through exercise and assignment. Additionally, we said that the further before the expiry date, there is even more reason for the option holder not to exercise. This means that the risk of being assigned is minimal but becomes more likely as the expiration date approaches and is most likely to happen when a dividend payment is at stake.

Options expire on the third Friday of their expiration month, and most of the assignments happen in the last few days of the week since it is when options have little "time value." If you're a seller and want to avoid being assigned, you should close out the option (with a "buy to close" order) before the likelihood of being assigned increases.

Here are some facts that illustrate why there is little reason to worry about being assigned. In 2016, of all the options, only about 7% were exercised and therefore assigned before the expiration date. This means that 93% of options were not exercised in the market. To sum up, one should not fear assignments because they rarely happen.

Up to now, we have discussed two ways an option contract can be ended: through the exercise and assignment procedure or through closing the position.

The final way one's option position can end is when it is allowed to expire worthlessly. If this happens, the option will simply disappear from the account. Obviously, one should only allow this to happen if there is no money to be made from the option contract. In this scenario, the premium paid stays with the seller. If you are the buyer, you have made a loss. If you are the writer, you get the premium the buyer paid and can keep it as a profit.

4

PRICING

In this chapter, we will learn about the pricing of an option, also called the premium, which is paid by buyers of option contracts to the sellers, and the factors affecting it. Much of what has been discussed in previous chapters has also had a lot of relevance to the price structure, and therefore this chapter brings many of the strands previously discussed together. After reading this chapter, you should have an even better grip on the previous information.

By now, you will have a rough idea of what the premium is, but let's summarize it so we can easily build on it going forward.

An option's premium is its price in the market. It can also be explained as the amount the buyer and seller of the option will agree on for the transaction. So, if you want to purchase a call or a put option, you will always pay a premium for it that goes to the seller of that option contract. If you choose to sell an option, this is what you will be paid.

HOW DO PREMIUMS WORK?

Understanding the price of a premium can tell you a lot about an option and its underlying asset. With the proper knowledge about the factors that influence the price of a premium, you can better understand how your investments (in options) will fare over time.

There are two components that make up the price of a premium: Its intrinsic value and its extrinsic value.

Intrinsic Value

Essentially, the intrinsic value of an option contract is the difference between its stock price (the current underlying asset price) and the strike price. For example, if the investor purchased a call option with a strike price of $20 and the underlying asset is at $25, since if the option holder exercised the contract, he could make $5 (since he could buy the stock of $20 and sell it for $25), we say there is $5 of intrinsic value to this option. Because this is the case, the option price would be at least $5, and the intrinsic value of the premium would be $5.

In other words, the intrinsic value is how much "in the money" the option is. Therefore, only options that are indeed ITM have intrinsic value. Since OTM (Out of the Money) and ATM (At the Money) options have no intrinsic value, their premium will have $0 of intrinsic value.

Extrinsic Value

The extrinsic value of an option is any value other than the intrinsic value. The intrinsic value represents the current value of the option now, whereas the extrinsic value represents the value an option has because of the value it may get. This value is derived from the possibility that an option will gain intrinsic value if the underlying asset's price moves in the option holder's favor. To understand this further, we need to break down extrinsic value into its two major components. The first is "time value," which comes from the time left until expiration. It has value because the longer the time left, the more likely the underlying asset's price will move in the holders' favor. The second component of extrinsic value is the "implied volatility" of the option, which is caused by the implied volatility of the underlying asset. In brief, implied volatility is a metric traders use to predict how likely the price of an asset is to move. Although what implied volatility is and where it comes from will be explained in a moment, what is important to know now is that this is a metric that measures what the market believes about the potential price moves of an asset. The higher the implied volatility, the more the market expects the price to move and, consequently, the more chance the underlying asset has of having large swings in either direction. Once again, this has value because the higher the volatility, the higher the chances of the asset's price moving in the holders' favor.

The difference between the intrinsic value and the option premium can be used to calculate the extrinsic value. In an equation, the extrinsic value would look like this: Option Premium-Intrinsic Value = Time Value + Implied Volatility (which is the extrinsic value). It follows that the total price of an OTM's premium comes entirely from its extrinsic value, i.e., from the possibility of the option becoming "in the money" and intrinsically profitable.

Since both time value and implied volatility are only valuable in as much as they can lead to intrinsic value, by expiration, only intrinsic value is left.

TIME VALUE AND TIME DECAY

Let's dive into the concept of time value and the closely related concept of time decay. We've already had a stab at them in the above section, but let's dive deeper into these characteristics.

Time value is one of the factors in the premium of an option; it's the amount of value the option has due to the time left until the expiration date.

Since the longer the time until expiration, the greater the chance that the option will be in-the-money, it stands to reason that an option with a longer time until expiration will be more expensive than the same option with a shorter time until expiration. Thus the first option has more time value than the second. It, therefore, also follows that the time value of an option is constantly dropping because the time until expiry and hence the likelihood of the stock price changing before expiry are both decreasing — this is known as "time decay." In a hypothetical case of an option with two months until expiry that was purchased for $2.50, if nothing changes by the next month, i.e., the price of the underlying asset has not moved, and the volatility has not changed, the price of this option will still have decreased significantly because the time value which was there because of the chance of the stock price moving favorably before expiry has decreased since there is only half the time left.

Simply put, investors are willing to pay more (or pay higher premiums) for more time since it increases their chances of profiting from their contract. In contrast, if an option contract has less time remaining, investors will pay less since there is a lower likelihood of profiting.

In the last chapter, we explained that when one wants to exit an option position before the expiry date, it's generally better to sell the option rather than exercise it. Now it should be clearer what this time value is and why it is being lost when the option is exercised.

Time decay is the measure of how the passage of time affects the time value of the option contract. Time decay accelerates as the expiration date nears. This means that the closer the option contract is to the expiration date, the more its time value will decrease (especially when there are only 30 days left). Conversely, the more time left in the contract, the slower the time decay happens. So when we say that an option's time value is declining, we are also saying that the time decay is accelerating. An option will typically lose the first half of its time value in the first two-thirds of its life and the other half of its time value in the last third. Remember that time decay will always be negative since time only goes in one direction. Furthermore, time decay begins the moment an option contract is acquired.

IMPLIED VOLATILITY

We've mentioned implied volatility above as part of the extrinsic value of an option's premium. Now we'll delve further into implied volatility and how it relates to option premiums. For an investor, there are two volatilities that we need to understand: historical volatility and implied volatility. Historical volatility is, in simple terms, how much the underlying stock of an option has fluctuated over a one-year period. For example, a particular stock value could have been $200 in January, and exactly a year later, it could still be $200; however, it could have had a lot of volatility during the year. It could have gone down to $50 in June and then up to

$300 in October, only to come back to $200 in January. This particular stock would be considered historically volatile if this were the case.

Implied volatility, on the other hand, is not established based on the stock's historical price but instead on what the stock market believes (or implies) the volatility of the stock might be in the future. Option traders are more interested in implied volatility because it's what is coming and not what happened before.

Now, from where does this implied volatility come?

The stock market, in general, is very susceptible to investors' moods. This means that the stock market will mimic the overall sentiment of investors. For example, if a report comes out stating that the major companies in the market are slowing down, investors might try to withdraw their investments, which would cause the stock market to go down. Conversely, if there is good news about the stock market, investors will invest more, bringing the market up. So investors' sentiment is linked to how the market performs. As we've seen, options are always linked to an underlying asset; therefore, investors' beliefs about the stock or option will affect the option's price.

The relationship between implied volatility and option prices is based on the marketplace of options. More specifically, when more people write and purchase options, it means that they are expecting moves. Therefore when the price of options increases, it shows that many people are writing and selling. This tells us that the market (its participants) expects the price to move. This is why it is called "implied volatility," since it implies that there will be volatility in the stock even though it hasn't moved yet. The logic behind the price mechanisms and why the purchaser would pay more for the option is that the more chance there is of volatility, the more likely the option will reach its strike price and beyond.

It, therefore, follows that if implied volatility increases, the price of options also increases (if we assume that all other factors remain constant). The opposite is also true; if volatility decreases, then the price of options (again, if all other factors remain the same) decreases.

Now that we've seen the relationship between implied volatility (IV) and the option price, it would be a good time to look at what else IV tells an investor and how it is measured.

Implied volatility can help an investor estimate the range of movement of a specific stock. To understand this, we need to know that implied volatility is expressed as a percentage. If you remember your Statistics 101 class, you will know that a stock has a 68% likelihood over the course of 12 months of ending up within one standard deviation (don't worry if you don't recognize this term). For example, let's assume that a specific stock is trading at $40 and the implied volatility of the option contract is 20%. This tells us that the market believes (or there's a consensus) that within the next 12 months, there will be a positive or negative move of $8 on the current price (20% of $40 is 8). In turn, this tells us that the stock market believes there's a 68% chance that at the end of those 12 months, the stock will be between $32 and $48. By definition, the stock has a 16% chance of being below $32 and a 16% chance of being above $48.

As you can see, implied volatility can help you determine the probability that a stock will fall within a certain price range by 12 months. Truthfully months seem like a rather long time for an option contract since the most common expiration date is usually 30 to 90 days. For the short term, one can do a quick calculation to determine the standard deviation move in that period.

One standard deviation move = (Stock price x Implied volatility x $\sqrt{\text{days to expiration}}$) / $\sqrt{365}$. So, if you have the stock price, for instance, at $30, its implied volatility at 20%, and 30 days to expiration, using the formula above, you could find the standard deviation.

Implied Volatility Relative to Historical Volatility

We've mentioned historical volatility before. This is the past volatility of the stock as it moved in the past. Now the reason why historical volatility is important is that implied volatility does not necessarily give us the whole story; implied volatility tells us if the stock is (expected to be) volatile relative to the market; however, we also want to know if the implied volatility is high or low relative to its own history. For that, we need to calculate it relative to the historical volatility. Let's look at the two metrics used to calculate and read the asset's implied volatility relative to its historical volatility: implied volatility rank and implied volatility percentile.

The implied volatility rank, also known as the IV rank or IVR for short, measures the implied volatility now relative to the range of implied volatility that the asset has had over a certain time period (usually a year). This is because the IVR's equation allows us to compare the current asset's implied volatility with the implied volatility range of the asset over a certain period. This is what the IVR of a year looks like put into an equation:

Current IV - 1-Year IV Low / 1-Year IV High - 1-Year IV Low

Let's use some real numbers to make this clearer. The IVR for a 25% IV stock that for the last year had an IV range between 20%, and 40% would look as follows:

25% - 20% / 40% - 20% = 0.25 or 25%.

This IVR of the example above tells us that the difference between the current implied volatility and the lower implied volatility is only 25% of the entire IV's year range. Hence, the current IV is closer to the lower end of historical volatility. This knowledge is relevant when choosing a strategy, as explained below.

The implied volatility percentile gives the trader the proportion of days in the recent past when the asset's implied volatility was lower than the present implied volatility; it is another metric used to comprehend the implied volatility relative to its historical volatility.

To calculate the IV percentile, you need to know how many days the implied volatility was below the current implied volatility over the last year. You then divide this number by the number of trading days in the year (252, since a year, has 252 trading days).

Number of Trading Days Below Current IV / 252

For instance, let's say the current implied volatility of the stock is 30%, and in the last 252 trading days, there were 100 days below the current implied volatility. The formula would look like this:

100 / 252 = 0.3968 or 39.68%

This tells us that the stock's implied volatility was below 30% around 39% of the time in the last year. This means that the current IV of 30% is not the norm, and one can expect the IV to increase.

You don't have to understand these equations; you need to be able to read the values they produce.

Now, you may be asking (correctly): which one should I use? IV rank or IV percentile?

Although both can come in handy, IV rank only tells you part of the story when used against historical levels of implied volatility. As we've seen above, the IV rank allows us to see where the current implied volatility of an asset is when compared to the implied volatility range over a period (usually a year). The problem with IV rank is that if the implied volatility of the asset were unusually high for a short period of time, anything that followed would be considered a low IV relative to the entire year's range, even if it is actually a high IV relative to the asset's normal range for the vast majority of the year. In short, if the IV decreases after a peak, the implied volatility rank will be low even if the IV remains high relative to the rest of the year. The implied volatility percentile, on the other hand, considers the number of days any given IV reading was for, providing a considerably more reliable picture of implied volatility. The implied volatility percentile is, therefore, the better indicator of the two.

Understanding how options are priced is vital to making great investments. The price of an option is its premium, or what you have to pay to acquire the right to purchase or sell the underlying stock. The option premium consists of its intrinsic and extrinsic value. The intrinsic value can be calculated by finding the difference between the current stock price and the strike price. The extrinsic value is any other value remaining in the premium. To evaluate the extrinsic value further, we need to understand the concepts discussed in this chapter, such as time value, time decay, and implied volatility.

In the next chapter, we will delve more deeply into the price of options, but this time from a different angle. We will be looking at how certain variables affect the premium. These are the Greek values. Much like implied volatility, these concepts make the difference between a trader who can pinpoint the best strategies and those who can't.

5

THE GREEKS AND THEIR RELEVANCE TO THE PRICE

So far, we've covered how numerous variables, such as time and implied volatility, impact option pricing. Investors use what are known as the Greeks to analyze the influence of these and other variables on the price. They're named such because they're represented by Greek letters like delta, gamma, theta, and vega. These metrics alter and adapt dynamically in response to market developments. Let's take a closer look at the Greeks, one by one.

DELTA

The delta tells us, or measures, the change in an option's premium that results from a change in the underlying asset's price. For example, imagine you have two call options, one

OTM and one ITM. The first option has a delta of 0.35, while the second has a delta of 0.90. If an increase of $1 occurs in the option's underlying asset, you'll see an increase of $0.35 on the first option and $0.90 on the second. For call options, the value of the delta can be from 0 to 1, while for put options, the value of the delta can be between -1 and 0. The reason for these numbers is that call options have a positive relationship with the underlying asset and puts a negative relationship. This means - in the case of a call - that if the underlying security price goes up, so does the premium of the call. On the other hand, the premium of puts has a negative relationship with the underlying asset's price; meaning premiums decrease when the underlying asset goes up. So if there is a put option with a delta of -0.35 and another with a delta of -0.90, this will mean that with a $1 increase in the underlying asset's price, the first option's price will decrease by $0.35 and the second option's price by $0.90.

The delta will never go above 1.00 (for calls) or below -1.00 (for puts). This is because a delta of 1.00 will mean the option's price will increase by $1 with a $1 increase to the underlying's price, and the option will never be able to gain more value from the underlying's increase than the underlying itself.

The idea here is that the nearer the option gets to 1.00 or -1.00, the more it is beginning to behave like the asset itself. The reason options' premiums don't usually follow the underlying asset's price changes 1 to 1 is that options' premiums also price in the potential of the stock price to change (i.e., its extrinsic value). Therefore as the premium does get closer to 1.00 or -1.00 (when in-the-money) or closer to 0 (when out-the-money), this will be because the chance of price changes is getting smaller, and therefore, only intrinsic value will be left. As an example, as an option gets nearer to the expiry date and there is less chance for price changes in the underlying, the more the price will act like the asset itself and the closer the delta will get to 1.00 if it is an ITM call or to 0 if it is an OTM option.

For this reason, the delta can be used to assess the market-assigned probability of the option being in-the-money at expiration. Essentially, a Delta closer to 1.00 or -1.00 is an indication of greater intrinsic value which can be translated into a higher probability of being in-the-money at expiration — potentially because it already is in-the-money.

Therefore the delta is the most important Greek since it informs us a lot more about the option. It indicates the likelihood of an option being ITM on its expiration date. For example, if an OTM call option has a delta of 0.30, it has a 30% probability of being ITM at its expiration date.

Traders also utilize the delta when determining their directional risk (which way they need the market to go). If they are bullish on the underlying, they will want a positive delta, whereas if they are bearish, they will want a negative delta. This is necessary when using complex strategies that utilize more than one type of option. In such a case, the trader will want to add the delta of all the options together to ensure the final delta correlates with his trading goals, e.g., a positive delta if he is bullish. Using the delta in this way is even more important when building what is called a neutral strategy. This is when you expect the underlying's price to not move in either direction, but you place your positions to benefit from other factors that influence the price, such as a change in IV (implied volatility). In this case, you must ensure that the delta of all the options comes out as zero.

Other things to keep in mind regarding delta are: It tends to rise closer to expiration for near or at-the-money options (since any change is more likely to be permanent since the time for more changes is running out). It can change in response to changes in implied volatility (again, since implied volatility affects the chances of the price changing). And the delta isn't a constant figure, as explained in the next section about gamma.

GAMMA

Gamma is what traders use to measure the rate at which the delta changes when the price moves. This is because delta values are constantly changing (since the underlying asset's price is continually changing), and gamma is used to give the traders an idea of those changes and what they can expect in the future. For instance, if a certain asset is trading at $10 and the gamma of the option is 0.1 while the delta is 0.5, this tells us that every time there's a $1 increase in the underlying price of the asset, the delta will adjust by 0.1. Therefore, if the underlying asset's price goes up by $1 to $11, the option's delta goes up to 0.6.

As traders, we can use the gamma to understand how stable the delta is, allowing us to understand the chances an option has of reaching its strike price at expiration. For instance, if you have two options with the same delta, but one has a low gamma value and the other a high gamma value, this tells us that the option with the high gamma value might have more volatility since the rate of delta swings more. This will mean it's a higher risk-reward trade since a move in the underlying asset will have an oversized impact. This would not be particularly good for most common traders who want predictability. Essentially, the gamma tells us the stability of an option's probability since the delta is the chance of an option being ITM at its expiration date.

With gamma, the number is positive for long positions and negative for short options, regardless of whether they are calls or puts. With gamma, it is highest for options near the money and lowest for options deep out-of-the-money or deep in-the-money.

THETA

Theta is used to measure the effect of time decay on the premium of an option. As we've discussed before, time decay is the decrease of an option's time value through time (until its expiration date). The closer an option is to its expiration date, the more time decay accelerates since there's less time for the trader to profit. Because time always moves in the same direction, theta's number is always negative; it doesn't have a minus sign; instead, it's represented as a regular number that refers to the amount of money the option will lose by the next day. So 34.86 means it loses $34.86 a day, and 91.46 means it loses $91.46 a day. This time starts as soon as a trader buys the option, so the value of the option starts to fall immediately—all other variables being equal—until the expiration date.

It follows that theta is bad for option buyers and good for option sellers. You can picture this as an hourglass where the buyer's side is up and the seller's side is down, so as the sand moves down, the option's value is flowing into the seller's side.

It's important to remember that the theta value is higher (meaning a lot of time value is lost with every passing day) on short-dated options and on near-the-money options because they have more urgency for the underlying asset to move.

VEGA

With vega, a trader can measure the risk of how changes in the implied volatility of the underlying security affect the price (premium). Its number represents the price difference for every 1% increase in implied volatility.

Because greater volatility increases the chances of the option hitting the strike price, the higher the volatility, the higher the price of the option.

For example, let's say the value of an option is $8, while the implied volatility is 15%, and the vega is 0.11. This means when the implied volatility goes from 15% to 17%, an increase of 2%, the option's price will increase to $8.22 (2 x 0.11 = 0.22, so 8 + 0.22 = 8.22).

MINOR GREEKS

Although minor Greeks are used mainly by computer software when carrying out very advanced strategies, and you, as a trader, can easily neglect them, it is worthwhile to mention them briefly.

The minor Greek factors are a lot less significant and nuanced than the main ones and are, therefore, not used by most traders. For example, rho measures the change to an option price brought about by every 1% interest rate change. Other minor Greek symbols include epsilon, lambda, zomma, vomma, or ultima. Some of these affect the main Greeks, such as the delta.

In summing up these most important indicators, it is essential to include implied volatility (IV) in the list. Together they aid the investor by giving vital measurements of the risks involved, such as how sensitive a specific trade is to price fluctuations, the passage of time, and volatility fluctuations movements. They also help the investor plan which strategy to use to make the greatest profit.

Let's take a deeper dive into the IV as an example of how to utilize an indicator to make profits. First, the IV can help determine which strategy to consider. For example, suppose options are trading with low IV levels. In that case, one should consider buying strategies since as the IV reverts back to its average, this will lead to an increase in "implied volatility" value, which will benefit the buyer. On the other hand, if the IV levels are high, one should consider selling strategies since as the IV reverts back to its average, the value from "implied volatility" will decrease, benefiting the seller.

Furthermore, one can attempt to forecast when IV levels will reverse from their peak or bottom. One can do this by finding the historical peaks and bottoms of the above-mentioned IV rank or IV percentile. Additionally, to find the extremes of volatility in the market as a whole, one can use the standard VIX chart, which works by averaging the implied volatility values of near-dated near-the-money S&P 500 index options.

Another more technical use of the IV is to find options that are undervalued relative to their IV and then use a buying strategy, or conversely, to find options that are overvalued relative to their IV and then use a selling strategy.

As hinted at earlier, these indicators will become increasingly important when putting together more advanced strategies that use more than one option in a single position.

When putting together these positions, one is trying to benefit from a particular aspect of the price mechanics. For example, if an investor doesn't know what will happen with the price, he can still profit by being right about what will happen with the IV. Or an investor might want to benefit from time decay without being affected by price changes. In these cases, he will want to set up a neutral trade on price direction but one that can still benefit from time decay or IV changes. In these cases, since the investor has no opinion on which way the price will go, they will need to be able to read the deltas to have a delta-neutral position. For example, if the two call options have a 0.25 delta and there is one put, they need to ensure the put's delta is -0.50.

Additionally, the investor will need to be able to read the theta and vega to know to what degree the market expectations for these are the same or different from his own and to asses the risk-reward ratio for his trade. For example, a big Vega can mean investors make a lot of money if the trade goes their way, but it can also mean they can lose a lot quickly should the trade not go their way. A big theta is desirable to an investor trying to benefit from selling options. Straddles and strangles described in chapter 8 are classic examples of these types of strategies.

There is a quick general point about the Greeks that needs to be mentioned for clarity. While discussing option indicators, we have done so in a vacuum. For example, we wrote that a positive delta means that the price of an option will increase when the underlying's price increases. However, in the real market, this doesn't always happen. This is because another factor can cancel out the rise in value to the premium, e.g., the decrease in value caused by the time decay (theta) might be bigger than the value increase caused by the delta.

A classic case where traders are not careful with this is when they purchase options on stocks that are having earning calls soon. They do this with the assumption that the extra trading volatility that happens in the lead-up to the earnings call in anticipation of announcements and surprise results will lead to an increase in options prices (i.e., a rise in IV). However, many don't take into account that the value lost by the time decay (theta) very often counters any gains in price from the increasing IV so that the actual price of the option goes down.

6

THE GENERAL RULES OF A GOOD TRADER

Investors need to follow many unwritten rules to become good at what they do. The first thing, perhaps the most important of them all, is the right mindset. Having the correct attitude will bring more advantages and opportunities when it comes to trading options.

THE PSYCHOLOGY OF INVESTING AND ITS IMPORTANCE

As you know, there are many skills and considerable knowledge that you need to have to be a successful investor. Things like the capacity to understand and evaluate a company's fundamentals and the ability to understand which direction a stock might go in the future. However, none of this matters if you don't have a great investor's mindset. This has hardly anything to do with your understanding of the stock market, options, thetas, or deltas. It has to do with your emotions and how you are able to manage them and with being able to think quickly and clearly when you're under pressure and things might not be going your way.

When it comes to emotions, there are two main ones that you need to have under control at all times: greed and fear. We will get to these emotions in a minute and how they play out when you're trading. However, first, we need to mention another important term: discipline. This discipline will keep your emotions in check.

It's obvious that to be a perfect trader, you need to have the ability to think quickly and often make fast decisions, getting in and out of trades with very little time. To do this correctly and adequately is impossible. Therefore to get the best results, one needs an arsenal of essential weapons, such as plans for all possible situations, the right habits and characteristics, and other ideas that will be mentioned. However, the string that pulls these all together is discipline. Because it can be easy to know your plan or the right mentality, but you need to have the proper discipline to be able to act on this knowledge.

Fear As an Investor

When investors receive negative news about the economy or about particular stocks, they tend to fear it. The first thing that often crosses their mind is to sell all their holdings and withdraw all their investments. When they do this, they might indeed avoid some losses, but as with most actions taken because of emotions, the chances are they will end up losing more when, for example, the position moves back up. To solve this, it helps to quantify fear and think about what makes investors fearful. However, this thinking should happen before any bad news arrives, not when you're going through it. By thinking ahead about these fears, traders can analyze what they might do when such events occur and what their reactions might be. This way, they are better equipped to deal with their instinctive and emotional responses. Obviously, this is easier said than done, but it's something that every investor must try to work at.

Greed As an Investor

Greed as an investor is the opposite of fear. Many investors and traders have the habit of holding on to a winning position way past the point at which their research could justify it. When the winning trend reverses, they end up losing the gains that they calculated correctly. Greed can sometimes be even harder to conquer than fear. It's also an instinctive behavior, but you, as an investor, need to be able to ignore this greed. The best solution is to invest following a plan that has already been worked out using a rational foundation.

SETTING THE RULES

As has been mentioned, one of the most important rules of being a successful investor is creating and setting rules based on rational thinking ahead of time. This way, the decision is not in your hands, or better yet, it's not in your hands when you're stressed or in a highly emotional state. These rules should be based on your personal tolerance for risk and reward, which in turn will be based on your individual needs. When you're setting your rules, you should also anticipate potential events, such as earnings releases, that could affect your position. Below are several ideas that can and should be used to improve one's planning and discipline.

RISK MANAGEMENT

Risk management is an important concept when planning your strategy because it will help you cut down on losses and ultimately help you find the right opportunities too. This section will discuss some of the most commonly used strategies for risk management and protecting your assets.

The key to risk management is knowing when to exit a trade before you even get into it. Not knowing when to sell is the biggest culprit for investors losing more than they had to on a losing trade and losing their profits on a winning trade. Often, when investors' positions start losing value, hope that the position will come back up kicks in. This typically ends with manageable losses becoming devastating losses. On the other hand, often, when investors' positions start to gain, they feel like they can't sell since if they do, the position might still go up, and they will have missed out on that opportunity. This, too, typically ends with the investor losing his original winnings. For this, you can use two methods to plan ahead: stop-loss (S/L) and take-profit (T/P). A stop-loss is a unique type of order that allows you to sell (or purchase back, in the case of an options seller) a specific option or stock when certain conditions you previously set are met. The order is carried out without you having to place it when the conditions are fulfilled. Instead, the conditions themselves will trigger the sale. All brokers will have this feature. This is an excellent tool to avoid further losses on a certain security because when one purchases the option (for, say, $3.00), they can already decide at what price they want out (for instance, they can make a sell stop-loss order for $1.50).

The truth is that although with stocks, this is a highly recommended idea, with options, it is not. Many professional investors believe that since options are potentially so volatile and can have very big swings in short periods, one should never place an automatic stop-loss order on them from the outset. Instead, before the trade, one should make a mental commitment to a stop-loss in time. This means choosing a time near expiration that if his original goals are still not in reasonably close sight, he will sell to save whatever value there may be left. One can adopt these ideas to keep gains by using a trailing stop-loss described later in the book.

A take-profit order is the opposite of a stop-loss; when you enter such an order, you specify the price the option has to reach for the take-profit order to trigger the action of closing the position. The take-profit takes away the risk of losing profits that have already been gained in a way similar to a stop-loss. It sells when you reach your predetermined target without allowing your emotions, such as greed, to get in the way. It's common for investors to use both a stop-loss and a take-profit order when investing. When you use these techniques, you are planning ahead, and you know precisely when you must exit a position. Most importantly, you take the decision out of your own hand by automating it beforehand.

From here, you can also evaluate the possible returns and the probability of the stock price hitting the goals you've set out. This is because you already know your maximum loss, i.e., the point chosen as the stop-loss. You will also know your maximum gain, i.e., the point selected as your take-profit.

In fact, for investors and traders that utilize technical analysis, stop-loss and take-profit points are typically set according to what the technical analysis tells the trader. Technical analysis is an entire subject on its own, so later on, we have given some technical analysis techniques that are relevant to options.

For someone not familiar with technical analysis, they can choose an arbitrary number as their sell point. This is because the important thing is to have a point where discipline takes over from the investor's current decision, which is subject to much emotion.

Investors that enter positions without these boundaries being defined are pretty much gambling in the sense that their emotions start to play a dominant role in their strategy.

Allocation

The 1% rule is an important one that you should consider. This rule states that traders should invest at most 1% of their money, or trading account, into a single option trade. For example, if you have $20,000 in your account, you should not invest more than $200 on one option trade. Obviously, this is an arbitrary number, but the point is that one shouldn't assume too much risk with any one option trade since losing one's entire investment isn't rare.

Diversity

You've undoubtedly heard the expression, "don't put all your eggs in one basket." This defines exactly what diversity in the stock market is. Diversifying your investments across the stock market by investing in different sectors, industries, regions, and market capitalizations assures that the overall damage is limited should one stock or sector's prices go against you. Besides minimizing your risks, diversification can also give you more opportunities to profit.

Other Risk-Management Strategies

Rebalancing your portfolio is a good way to avoid risks. For instance, imagine that you've got a strategy in place and have allocated your investments properly. After some time, you will find that certain investments weigh more than others. This is when the rebalancing comes in.

When you rebalance your portfolio, you purchase and sell parts of it to set the weight of the different assets you have back to where they were when you started investing. This is done in order to recapture your initial risk-reward strategy. This means selling some of your winners and using that money to purchase more of the positions that have grown less. If your strategy has changed, you can rebalance your portfolio to reflect this new strategy.

The frequency you rebalance your portfolio depends on many factors, such as your account type, transaction costs, taxes, and goals.

Sometimes losing positions need to be let go. At times, hope is what keeps us moving and is a source of belief, making us hold onto positions we shouldn't hold. However, the stock and options market is a cold and sober place where only facts matter. If there's no good news when you look at the evidence and the numbers of a losing stock, you have to be rational and logical and pursue other paths. There will be instances where you have to give in and sell your stock at a loss before it continues to go down.

The Risks of Too Much Margin

As previously stated, when selling options, one's loss potential is limitless. As a result, the brokerage will request a margin. It is critical to comprehend the significance of this. The broker requires the investor to put up assets as security for this trade. The collateral is required in the event that the transaction results in large losses, and the brokerage must now ensure enough cash to cover the losses. They will subsequently sell these extra assets to raise the required funds. This illustrates how selling options carries a high level of risk. What should be a single losing trade can turn into losses on multiple positions.

LOGGING YOUR TRADES

Logging your trades is a great way to keep up with the trades that you make. You write down every transaction that you make and when you exit them. It might not seem like much, but it can help you understand the performance of your trades, allowing you to understand what you're doing right and what you're doing wrong. This is essential if you want to improve your game, especially because everyone makes mistakes, and how are you to learn from them if you don't write down what you have done? When you don't keep a record of everything you've done, you are likely to continue to make the same mistakes over and over again, which will compound your losses in the long run.

You need to start making this a habit to identify your errors better. Logging your trades will also bring the desired discipline you need when trading options.

If you care about statistics, you definitely should keep a log. By logging in to your trades, you can have a clear overview of important stats. You can quickly check the number of trades you've made, your wins and losses, your risk and reward ratios, and other important information.

Setting Up and Using a Trade Log

Here are a few essential things you will want to keep track of when keeping a trade log.

The symbol of the underlying stock, the expiration date, what type of option play it is, e.g., a call or a put, the entry date, the exit price, the premium you paid, the total holding period for your winners, and your losses, and your profits and losses.

This is the essential data in any options trading log. However, here are other pieces of information that can be very helpful to add. For instance, depending on your strategy, you can add the Greeks of each option. Implied volatility, IV percentile, and margin are other options for parameters that you can add to get a larger picture of your trading.

As part of logging your trades, it's important that you ask yourself a few questions. For example, "What made you perform this trade in the first place?", "What was the result of the trade?", "How successful did you think the trade was going to be, and how did it live up to your plan?" and "What did you learn from this particular trade?"

BACKTESTING

Backtesting is an excellent way of understanding how well a particular model would have succeeded if it was indeed used in the past. By using historical data, backtesting allows us to estimate how a certain trading strategy will work in the future. Past success doesn't indicate whether or not a certain trade or stock will succeed in the future. However, if a certain strategy has worked in the past, it is likely to work in the future.

Backtesting uses data coupled with tools to provide statistics about a given strategy. To do this, one will need to use backtesting software, where one can customize their settings to include whatever data they would like to use.

PAPER TRADING

Paper trading is when investors practice trading without real money. When online trading didn't exist, investors had to use actual paper to practice their trading by recording every transaction and checking their results. Nowadays, you have online stock simulators that bring you closer to the real stock market.

Most brokerage companies nowadays offer these services, but it's better to check what other tools within the "paper trading world" they offer so you can have a much closer real-life experience. For instance, TD Ameritrade has great paper trading software called PaperMoney, that allows investors to try out strategies using options too.

A good place to start is using a market simulator to get familiar with order types such as stop-losses, take profits, sell-to-close orders, etc. Paper trading is a great idea for practice and is also used by experienced traders when they have new strategies they want to introduce.

CHARACTERISTICS OF A WINNING TRADER

Being a great trader is more than just having a great strategy. You need to have certain characteristics to become good at what you do.

Discipline

As already discussed earlier, discipline is the most important trait a trader needs. There are many options on the market, and it's easy to get overwhelmed or even enticed by some of them to the point that you'll follow them without proper reasoning just because they look great. However, only some opportunities you will face will give you the desired returns. Beginner traders often fall for rookie mistakes such as over-trading, following the wrong trades, exiting trades too early, or holding them for longer than they should. If the trade in front of you doesn't follow your designed strategy, you should not go for it. This requires discipline. When no opportunities fall into your strategy, you are required to do absolutely nothing; this is where discipline comes in. Being able to sell when necessary also needs discipline.

Patience

Being patient is often linked to being disciplined because being a trader requires you to wait for the right opportunity. When you have a strategy in place, it's easier to understand the right time to take action. Most of the time, you will have to be patient, analyzing each potential opportunity without you forcing it.

Adaptability

Being able to adapt to the different circumstances of the market quickly is also a great attribute to acquire as an investor. This means being prepared for all market conditions, such as a sudden change from a bull market to a bear market, when one's overall strategy and specific strategy to find opportunities will have to change considerably.

Mental Durability

Even if you stick to your approach as an investor, you will make bad trades from time to time. It happens all the time to both new and seasoned investors. You must be mentally tough to recover from this situation. When things don't go your way, it's natural to feel dispirited. A key difference between successful and unsuccessful traders is their capacity to keep pushing forward and reviewing their approach.

Winning and losing streaks will happen, but you need to keep your focus in either case. You can't be excessively excited about winning or completely discouraged about losing. You have to keep your balance and stay focused on your overall goal. How one behaves and acts after highs and lows will define them as an investor; being mentally tough and focused is key to accomplishing that.

Being Independent

Although when you're starting, you will need help and tips from others, ultimately, you will be the one that makes the decisions.

You will have to establish your independence from these sources at some point. Once you've established your strategy, you will want to follow it regardless of what others think. This will lead to you constantly feeling that you don't know enough and practically being too afraid to go at it on your own. Acquiring independence doesn't mean you don't get to ask for help or look for answers. On the contrary, being an investor means constantly looking for new ways to improve yourself and acquire knowledge. Independence means confronting yourself and recognizing that you must take responsibility for your own results.

HABITS OF A WINNING TRADER

Traits are not the only thing you should strive to improve; you also need to create good habits as a trader. Good habits, with great mentality and traits, can get you very far with investing. Habits are routine actions you perform throughout your investing career that can help you stay on track.

We've already mentioned what keeping a journal and logging your trades can do for you as an investor, but there are many more habits that you can create to help you perform better.

Continue to Seek Knowledge

You will never know everything. However, if you want to be a successful trader, you must continue to study as much as possible and create the habit of wanting to learn more about other strategies or new developments in the industry. Warren Buffett is well-known for reading up to six hours every day—that's not bad company!

Treat Your Investments Like a Business

You have to get in the habit of treating your investments like a business - because they are! You are trying to make a profit and balance out your expenses with your earnings. Make sure you write down a business plan complete with a strategy, routines, and daily tasks so you can keep up with everything that comes your way during your trading day.

Learn How to Use Tools

Nowadays, brokers provide a plethora of tools you can take advantage of; it has never been easier to make results happen. This aligns with always seeking more knowledge and treating investing like a business. Good investors make a habit of using the best tools available to them.

Review Your Trades

Successful investors analyze their trades regularly. This is because they understand that only by practicing and going through their trades to examine their actions will they be able to determine what they did correctly and what has to change for the next time.

TECHNICAL ANALYSIS WITH OPTIONS

When trading options, time is of the essence. This is because, with options, it is not enough only to estimate the direction and price of the underlying asset but also precisely when it will occur. For example, if you predict that stock ABC, which is currently at $90, will hit $100, and you go ahead and buy the $95 call option with the first of February expiry date, and indeed the stock does go from $90 to $100 as you predicted. If this happens the day after the first of February (your expiry date), you will not have made a penny. On the contrary, you will have lost your entire capital spent on the premium. Here is where technical analysis comes into play. The ability to interpret charts to anticipate where prices will go and when they will arrive is known as technical analysis. This means that, besides being able to predict the price, technical analysis can also help one predict when that price might be reached.

The basic logic behind why charts work is that people trade with emotions, and it is these emotions that the charts can predict. For example, if a chart shows that the share price is having a hard time breaking $100, the chart will show that this is a difficult emotional barrier for traders to cross.

In terms of using this knowledge to predict the price, an investor may buy the stock at a lower price, say $92, and then sell it at $99 before the price reverses. If trading options, he could buy the $95 call and sell it when the underlying nears $100. Once the stock price reaches $100, he may decide to make money from the declining stock price with another strategy. For example, he can buy a $100 put option when the stock price is $99, believing it will get resisted again and go down. In this case, the investor will also be able to pick a stop-loss since he knows that if the stock price breaks through $100, his reasoning is wrong, and he has no reason to hold the position anymore. Therefore, when the stock price goes to $101, he will sell his option and cut his losses. (Practically, the numbers will not be that neat, and a stock price being rejected at $100 merely implies that it will hit around that level, albeit it may occasionally go over to $101 or $102 or whatever, so the stop loss will be higher than $101 and will depend on historical data.)

It should be apparent from this that when it comes to options trading, understanding how to see trends and read the volatility, volume, and momentum of the underlying asset is a great benefit for someone wanting to make solid returns. This doesn't mean that one who can't read technical analysis can't trade options; it just means that one should be aware of their limits and trade accordingly. For example, they should give themselves more time, so if they know a stock is going up in the near future, they should look at buying a call with a strike price at least six months away. As a general rule, the quicker you want the move to be, the more you will need to understand technical analysis.

As mentioned earlier in the book, technical analysis is an entire subject unto itself, and there are literally hundreds of different technical indicators that traders have come up with over the years. For that reason, we'll only scratch the subject's surface and concentrate on the specific aspects that are more relevant to options trading.

Let's start with trendlines. Trendlines are easily recognizable lines that investors draw on charts to connect a series of prices together. One draws a line connecting all the price peaks (usually, it will be across all the highs for a downtrend and all the lows for an uptrend) for the time frame in which they are interested. This will then clearly show the investor the trend of the price action (since the lines will show the direction that the stock is trending). These lines give investors an idea of where the stock price is going. When drawing trendlines, you can have three possible outcomes: a downtrend, an uptrend, and a sideways trend.

When you have a downward trendline, it usually tells you that investors are more willing to sell than to purchase. This also tells us that the stock will potentially continue to go downward. When looking at a downtrend, it is helpful to check if there is a series of lower lows in addition to the lower highs that the trend line was drawn above. If there is, this further confirms the downtrend. On the other hand, an uptrend means there's more buying than selling, and stocks in that category tend to continue to go upward. Once again, if there are also a series of higher highs in addition to the higher lows that the uptrend was drawn below, this confirms the uptrend.

You need to look at trendlines from a time frame point of view since these can change significantly. For instance, you might have some assets that have been performing in a downtrend or uptrend for weeks or days, but when you zoom out, you find out that they are actually going the opposite way.

The third possibility is that an asset might be moving in a sideways trend. This means that the price is going horizontally, and so buying and selling are balanced. This is usually temporary, and the stock price is most likely going through a consolidation period before it changes trendlines.

The common investing adage that sums up the importance of understanding trends is "The trend is your friend."

Resistance and Support

Other important information to be drawn from trendlines is the identity of areas of support and resistance. Support and resistance points tell us at which prices the stock price may stop falling or have difficulty passing. Specifically, the support line tells us where the stock price might not fall below (hence the name "support"), while the resistance line indicates the value that the stock price might not surpass (hence the name "resistance"). Support and resistance points are only temporary and are, therefore, only predictions and probabilities.

These are significant to investors because they help to determine when to enter a position and where to set stop-loss and take-profit orders. When the stock price gets near a trendline, it usually does one of two things. It either hits the trendline and bounces off of it (meaning that it hits the resistance or support point and continues in the same trendline direction), or it passes through the trendline, indicating that a new trend is forming. This gives the investor multiple possibilities about how he will want to trade this. He may want to place a position betting on the price bouncing off the trendline (which is the most probable event, all things being equal), in which case the trader will also have a price that he can set as a sell-stop. If the price doesn't rebound but goes through the trendline, he knows that his trade didn't work out, and he has no more justification for keeping the trade open.

On the other hand, if he believes that this time there is a reason for the price to break the trendline, he will trade differently. For example, if the trendline suggests that the price shouldn't go over $90, he might wait for the price to go to $92 and then buy in, assuming the price will now keep going in this direction. In this case, he could use previous trendlines for this asset to suggest price targets. For example, if, in this case, the price used to trade in a range with $100 as the resistance, he can assume that the price will get to around $100 before being rejected again. With this knowledge, he can also set a take-profit at this point ($100). Practically he can't set this up beforehand since he doesn't know the price the option will be when the underlying hits his target. This will have to be a mental commitment to sell his option when the underlying stock reaches this price.

Drawing trendlines is relatively easy. You can quickly identify a stock's high and low prices, and as noted before, when looking at an up-trending stock, you draw the line by linking the support points/low prices. When analyzing a downtrend, you draw the line by linking the high prices that behave as the resistance points. Ultimately there is some subjectivity since, with all patterns, it can seem one way to one person and another way to another. It is also your decision on whether to use closing or open prices.

It is important to know that the more times the price is tested and still holds, the more influential the support and resistance are.

TECHNICAL INDICATORS FOR OPTIONS TRADING

Having discussed trendlines, let's turn to specific technical indicators relevant to options traders. Many of these indicate overbought and oversold levels. These are relevant to option traders because when looking at an oversold or overbought stock, you can expect a price reversal in the near future, and as already mentioned, success in trading options depends on getting the timing right.

Relative Strength Index (RSI)

The relative strength index, or RSI, measures when a security is overbought or oversold. The RSI values range between 0 and 100. When the number is 70 or above, it is considered an indication that the asset is overbought. If the value is 30 or below, it is to considered to be an indication that the asset is oversold. It works by comparing the magnitude of recent gains to recent losses over a given period of time to measure the security's speed and change of price movements in an attempt to determine whether the conditions are overbought or oversold.

This momentum indicator usually works better when analyzing options on individual stocks than with options on indexes (that track more than one stock).

Bollinger Bands

Bollinger bands measure volatility increases and decreases—something we already know to be important when dealing with options trading—as a way of adapting to price expansions and contractions. Practically speaking, when looking at a chart with Bollinger bands added, one will see three lines going through the chart; the top and bottom lines are the actual Bollinger bands, and the middle one is a simple moving average (SMA). The SMA tells us the asset's average price over a certain period of time. The bands create a boundary on either side of the SMA, showing where the price is overbought (when near the top band), and where oversold (when near the bottom band). The bands will be narrow if the stock price has a narrow range. The bands will be wide if the stock price has a wide range of volatility.

Bollinger Bands can be used in a few ways. One common way traders use it is to indicate when a price reversal is due. This would be the case if the price of a stock moved outside the bands. The bands can be used at a basic level to confirm a trend.

Money Flow Index (MFI)

The momentum flow index uses data such as volume and price to understand the influx and outflux of cash in a specific stock over time (usually 14 days). It gives what traders call "trading pressure." Because it uses volume data as an important parameter, this momentum indicator is better used in individual stocks and long-term trades. Ultimately, this indicator, which is evaluated between 0 and 100, tells us if a stock is oversold or overbought. Anything below 20 indicates that the stock may be oversold, while anything above 80 indicates that it may be overbought.

The MFI can also offer us a heads-up and alert us if the stock's trend is shifting. This is when there are divergences. A divergence occurs when, for example, the stock continues to rise but the indicator changes to suggest that there is now a lot less volume than before. This shift in volume may be an early signal that the price will move shortly as well. As with the previous indicators (because you can find this one as a tool in many brokerage charts), you don't need to know how to calculate it; instead, you simply need to learn how to interpret it.

Put-Call Ratio Indicator (PCR)

This is quite a simple indicator to understand, as it measures the volume of trades that use call options against the trades that use put options to gauge the market's overall sentiment. If there are more calls than puts, this indicates bullish behavior and is expressed by a ratio above one. On the other hand, if there are more puts than calls, this indicates bearish behavior, and the ratio is shown as less than one.

Open Interest (OI)

The open interest indicator shows the number of option contracts that are not closed or settled (exercised). Although this indicator doesn't tell you where a trend will go, it's useful in understanding a trend's force. When there's a growing interest (when the OI increases), this means there's more money coming in, which in turn tells us that the trend is getting stronger. If there's a decrease in open interest, the trend is getting weaker.

Following the above logic, one can use the OI and price move in the following ways. If both the OI and the stock price rise, this tells us that the particular stock is strong. If the stock price rises but the OI is decreasing, this can mean that although the price is still going up, the stock is weakening. If the stock price is falling and the OI is increasing, in this case, this tells us that the particular stock is very weak (since the OI shows a lot of interest in positions that predict a decreasing stock price). If both are falling, although the particular stock price is still going down, the stock is strengthening.

There are many more technical indicators you can use to predict the direction of the underlying assets of your options. Starting with these can give you a solid grounding in momentum indicators. You don't have to use all the indicators we've discussed. They are just some common ones that are good starting points. With time and experience, you'll be able to adjust your strategy and pick the best ones to complement that strategy.

FUNDAMENTAL ANALYSIS WITH OPTION TRADING

Unlike technical analysis, where traders and investors use technical indicators to tell them what the market is thinking about any given asset, fundamental analysis is about the investor researching and getting information about the objective reality of the company's intrinsic worth and, by extension, its prospects. The idea is that if the critical underlying aspects that a company requires to be successful are solid, then even if the company isn't trading well right now, the market will eventually come to appreciate it, and the stock price will rise accordingly. The distinction between fundamental and technical analysis can be summarized as follows: Fundamental analysis seeks to determine what to purchase, whereas technical analysis determines when to buy it. Additionally, as an extension of this, fundamental analysis is more important when looking for long-term positions, whereas technical analysis is more important if one intends on only holding a position for a short time.

So, now that we've established that fundamental analysis focuses on determining a company's intrinsic value, what is that value? It is how much the firm is worth based on its current cash flow and, more importantly, its projected cash flow. In principle, the market price of a company's shares is what investors are willing to pay because of the cash income the shares represents (either now or in the future). Therefore, looking at a company's intrinsic worth implies considering its previous financial success and potential to produce money.

To make a fundamental analysis of a company, the first thing investors should do is understand the current general economic environment. For this, you need to zoom out and try your best to understand the macroeconomic environment, such as rising inflation or interest rates, and any global or domestic events that might affect the stock price. For instance, if you're looking at a company that relies on acquiring materials from a foreign country, you will need to know each country's economy and currency strength. You also need to be aware of that foreign country's political and geopolitical situations to understand if anything is blocking the transfer of materials, whether because of national political uncertainty or war.

Once you've cleared that step, the next thing to do is look at the company itself and perform deep research. You're looking to understand everything you can about the company: the way it operates, the way it makes money, what its business model is, etc. Analyzing the financial statements is a good start. The most significant ones to look at are the income statements, balance sheets, and cash flow statements. Look back at least two years to better understand how the company is performing. The easiest way to look for the company's financial statements is to go to its website since all publicly-traded companies must disclose them. When you're analyzing the company, you need to look for positive signs of growth, any advantage it might have compared to other competitors in the industry, and the quality of its management.

The last step is to choose the company's top competitors and perform a similar analysis by looking at their financial statements and comparing them to the one you're analyzing. Can you explain why you want to invest in your chosen company? Can you articulate its edge or its unique selling point over its competition?

Although fundamental analysis is more important for investors looking to make long-term investments, such as LEAP options (which are long-term options as explained later), it is critical to know that the fundamentals of any company you invest in - no matter how long you plan on holding the investment - are solid.

UNDERSTANDING TICKER SYMBOLS

Now that you are ready to trade options, let's walk through how to identify an option contract's necessary information from its ticker. The ticker is a unique combination of letters and numbers that correspond to a stock or security; each asset has its own unique ticker. Before 2010, it wasn't easy to identify options by their ticker symbol since there was no unanimity. In 2010 the Options Clearing Corporation (OCC) released the Options Symbology Initiative (OSI) so that now by looking at an options ticker, you can easily understand what option you're looking at.

While stocks' ticker symbols only have a couple of basic letters (and sometimes the odd number) to identify them, options have both letters and numbers that give us a little more information about them. The format goes like this: First comes the root symbol that corresponds to the stock; second is the expiration date; then the identifier, whether it's a put or a call; and last, the strike price.

Usually, you will have up to 21 characters, both letters, and numbers. Let's have a look at this Apple call. The ticker symbol is "AAPL220826C00075000." The first four letters are the ticker symbol for Apple. The following six digits tell us about the expiry date, which is the twenty-sixth of August (i.e., 08) 2022. Next, the letter "C" identifies this as a call option, and finally, the last piece of information is that the strike price is $75. This one is not so clear because of all the eight digits. However, divide the last eight numbers by 1,000, and you will get the right strike price.

In summary, there are many rules to follow to become a successful options trader.

The first thing any investor needs to aim for is a good psychology and mindset towards options and the market in general. To mitigate negative emotions that still arise, having a good set of rules in place based on a rational plan that you follow with discipline is the key.

In line with this, technical analysis has an important role in helping draft trading plans and choosing sell-stop prices through the use of trendlines, support and resistance levels, and momentum indicators such as the Relative Strength Index and Bollinger bands, etc. In line with being a mature investor with a mindset of always being thirsty to learn more, fundamental analysis should also not be ignored.

Additionally, nurturing good habits and characteristics will make you more assertive and rational when placing your trades. Some traits might not come naturally to you, and you will need to work on them actively. The same goes for habits you are not used to performing, such as logging and reviewing trades. Although the effect of much of this isn't immediately apparent, over the long term, an investor will be able to look back and see how, indeed, this was the key to his success!

7

GETTING THE MOST OUT OF OPTIONS CONTRACTS

In this chapter, we'll start talking about the different ways that you can use options contracts. We'll go through ways in which you can benefit from specific types of options contracts, such as index and ETF options, as well as look at some basic strategies you can apply when trading options.

INDEX AND ETF OPTIONS

Before we go through what index and ETF options are, we'll first briefly introduce what index funds and ETFs entail in general.

Index funds are a type of mutual fund since they are made up of many different people's money, which is then invested in many different stocks. What makes them unique is that these funds aim to track certain segments (i.e., indexes) of the stock market by bringing many stocks together into a single portfolio. One of the most popular ones is the S&P 500 index, which tracks the 500 largest publicly-traded companies in the U.S. There are many index funds that track almost every segment of the stock market. Exchange-traded funds (ETFs) are in many ways the same as index funds in that they are also made up of many individual stocks that track indexes. The difference between index funds and ETFs is in how they are traded. ETFs can be traded just like you would trade any individual stock in the market, while index funds can only be bought at the price set at the end of the day. So, while all indexes are mutual funds, not all mutual funds are index funds, and not all index funds are ETFs.

GETTING STARTED

There are many reasons for you to want to expand your opportunities when it comes to options trading. Index (including ETF) options are a great place to start. The benefits of trading index options come from the diversity they offer since the underlying of the option is a diversified index. Having this diversification means a couple of things. First of all, there is less risk since, as pointed out earlier, when there are many positions, if one of them indeed has a large price decline, the other positions will save you from the full force of the loss. Of course, this also means your gains won't be massive either. Suppose there is a significant market event for one of the underlying assets, such as a merger or surprise earnings report. In that case, the impact will also be much smoother because you are trading with many underlying stocks. However, this is also a benefit because it results in low overall volatility in the option. Indeed they are very popular amongst investors and an excellent place to start for beginners since they offer many of the benefits of options without the volatility normally associated with options. Additionally, this minimal volatility will also translate into much cheaper premiums.

Another benefit of trading index options is that they offer more liquidity (this refers to how quickly you can purchase and sell an option or stock), which makes the bid-ask spread narrower. The bid/ask spread is the difference between someone's willingness to purchase and someone else's willingness to sell. The benefit of this is simple. When you want to make a purchase, there is a greater chance of there being someone else who will agree to your price.

Index Options vs. ETFs Options

The differences between index options and ETF options (especially if they track the same market segment) are generally small. You can have a large exposure to the market with a single trade in any of them. Let's have a look at the differences between index and ETF options.

Different Tax Treatment

When it comes to taxing your profit from your options, you are more likely to be better off with index options. When you trade ETF options, your earnings are considered short-term gains and are taxed at the ordinary income rate, which today can range from 10% to 37% (the exact amount you are taxed depends on your tax bracket).

If you hold index options for less than a year, you can still qualify for the 60/40 tax treatment (60% of your profits are taxed as long-term capital gains, while 40% of your profits are taxed as short-term capital gains). Using these advantageous tax treatments means you will be able to retain more of your gains. Not all index options fall into this category, so you may be unable to take advantage of it, but the Mini-SPX and Mini-RUT, which track the SPY and the S&P 500, can be used with this tax treatment, providing you with broad market exposure. Obviously, investors should consult with their tax advisors to determine how the profit and loss on any particular option strategy will be taxed and how it should be reported for tax purposes since tax laws and regulations change from time to time and may be subject to varying interpretations. Additionally, there may be certain criteria that need to be met.

Cash Settlement vs. Share Settlement

Another difference between index options and ETF options is the settlement style. With ETF options, you get physical shares of the underlying asset delivered, as with standard stock options. This gives you meaningful exposure to the market (physical share delivery means that the actual underlying security is to be delivered on the expiration date). With index options, however, you get a cash settlement (i.e., a cash payment).

With ETFs, where you get a share settlement, one thing to keep in mind is that this can increase the risk in your portfolio because you now possess shares that can fall in value. This is especially problematic if the expiration date is on a Friday (as is typically the case) since the price might fall over the weekend, so that by Monday, it may have lost value. However, with cash settlement, you have no further risk once the option expires because the money is sent directly into your account.

It should be pointed out, though, that as explained in Chapter 3, the owner of an option can always close the trade out before expiry. Therefore, even with an ETF option, if the holder wants cash instead of shares, he can sell the option for a profit without needing to accept any shares.

American vs. European Style Options

The last big difference between ETF options and index options is the option style. ETF options offer what are called "American-style options." This means that the option trader can exercise the option at any time before or on the expiration date (again, similar to standard stock options). In contrast, index options offer "European-style options," which means they can only be exercised at expiration.

As we've already discussed in Chapter 3, an option owner might want to exercise their option before the expiration date if there's an ex-dividend date approaching (if you recall, the ex-dividend date is a set date before the dividend, where if you own the shares, you will be paid the dividend). If this were the case, he would want to use ETF options that give him this possibility.

If you are a seller, perhaps going for an index option might be more prudent since this will mean that you don't have to deal with early assignments.

As you can see, both ETF and index options have their advantages and disadvantages, and choosing one over the other will depend on your style. However, one thing is sure, starting out with some index option (whether index or ETF) is very beneficial.

Notably, the portfolios of professionals make effective use of index and ETF options.

BASIC STRATEGIES WHEN BUYING CALLS AND PUTS

At the most basic level, the most straightforward strategy is to buy a call or a put. It should be stressed that just because something is basic doesn't mean it is unimportant. On the contrary, it is the foundation on which all other, more complex strategies are built, not to mention that it will be how you make your biggest wins. Additionally, each of these trades has an opposite side, the seller or writer of the contract. As has been mentioned, the seller's risk-reward ratio is very unattractive (since the gain is limited to the premium and the loss is unlimited in the case of call sellers and still very large for put sellers). Therefore options writing shouldn't be considered a basic strategy like simply buying calls or puts. However, this being said, it is also a fundamental strategy that brings with it a high probability of winning.

In the next chapter, we will discuss a strategy for selling options that will give the trader the same chance of winning while eliminating the unlimited loss potential.

Quickly some terms. You might have heard that purchasing a call is bullish behavior while buying a put is bearish. This is true because, like when we mention a "bull market," we define it as a market that rises over a certain period. So too, when you purchase a call, you can only profit from it if the underlying share price increases in value. A bear market happens when there is an extended price decline, so purchasing a put option is considered bearish behavior because you profit when the underlying share price declines in value.

Using Options for Hedging and Risk Management

As we've hinted at in previous sections of this book, hedging is a way to reduce a portfolio's risk from price declines. One uses options to hedge, and indeed hedging is one of the most common ways investors use options. Let's focus on put options and how to use them to hedge - first, a quick recap on how a put option works.

A put option gives the buyer the right, but not the obligation, to sell a specified underlying asset at a predetermined price at any given time up to the expiry date. When purchasing this contract, the buyer pays a premium. The put option contract will indicate what the asset is, what the exercise price is, and the expiration date. The seller of the put option gets the premium paid by the buyer, whatever the outcome, in return for obligating themselves to buy the underlying asset if the buyer exercises their right to sell it to them. When a put option is exercised, the buyer of the option is selling the underlying asset to the seller of the option contract for the amount specified on the contract, even if that means that the option seller is purchasing the asset at a much higher price than its current market value.

Following on from what has just been explained, let's look at an example of how you would use a put option to hedge. If you own, let's say, 100 shares of a $50 stock (a total of $5000) because you are ultimately bullish on the company, but you also want to protect yourself against a severe drop in the price because you believe there is a chance of the economy taking a bad turn. You can purchase a put option as a hedge in case of this sudden price decrease. In our example, this could mean that you buy a put with a strike price of $48 for $0.10 (adding to a total of $100 for all 100 shares). If, indeed, the market suddenly takes a hit and your shares fall by 10% to $45, if you didn't have any put options, this would have cost you $500 (10% of your initial $5000). However, now your puts give you the right to sell the shares for $48. This means that you will not lose money on your stock position by more than 4% (which is $200). Together with the original $100 spent on buying the options, this comes out to be $300. All in all, this means that you saved yourself losing an extra $200.

If the investor is worried about even more considerable losses, then hedging with puts will be more important. Ultimately, when hedging, you still prefer the stock price to increase, so you make more money through share appreciation. However, this is similar to an insurance policy where you don't actually want to need to take the insurance payout, and the insurance is just there in case of a disaster. Puts used in this way are called "protective puts." Big institutional investors do this when they believe the market/economy will see a turnaround. When they think a bull market is coming to an end and, because of the size of their positions, they can't offload all their shares without crashing the price, they will start to buy puts on the shares they own.

The average investor can actually use this information as an indicator of market sentiment. When one notices that there are suddenly many puts being bought but that the market is still rising, it should trigger a warning that the market may be in for a turnaround. Since the increase in puts is probably because of the institutional money buying them, this means that the institutions are predicting a turnaround for the market. If indeed this is their belief, it is worth your attention. One way of telling this is by looking at the VIX. The VIX rises when demand for puts increases. This means that when the VIX rises but the market is still rising, the increase in puts is probably being bought by big institutions that are predicting a market turnaround. Once again, if indeed this is their belief, pay attention.

To reiterate, you don't actually want to gain from these puts; instead, you want them to expire worthless because you would rather your long position do well (i.e., the $5000 you hold go up in value). The investor still purchases these puts because it is worth it for him to pay the premium for the protection they provide him against potential price slides. It is similar to the expense of paying insurance.

The catch here is that using puts to protect against a decline in your portfolio can end up being very expensive. As we've discussed earlier in the book, the option contract's premium depends on a few variables, such as the current market price of the underlying security, the time until the expiration date, the implied volatility, and other things. While puts can protect the value of your investments by making sure that the value doesn't go below the amount specified as the strike price in the put option (since you have the right to sell the security at that price), buying "protection" is expensive, and if you constantly use puts to hedge, your returns will diminish significantly due to the premiums you will be paying regularly (and volatile times can really make these expensive).

As an investor, you will be aware of the power of dividend compounding on long-term investments, where regularly adding in money and getting returns on your returns boosts your returns exponentially. By constantly purchasing puts, you are essentially doing the reverse of compounding by periodically decreasing your gains. You might think, then, that you should just buy puts when the market looks unsteady. That, too, is not the best idea because options are the most expensive in that environment since the implied volatility will be much higher. So when is the right time to purchase put options to mitigate risks? We don't have the correct answer because there is none. It is just important for the trader to be aware that, as with every situation, there are trade-offs, and one should try to only buy as much protection as necessary to not overly decrease returns.

What Can You Do About It?

There are strategies that you can use to be able to hedge and minimize the costs. One is called a "bear put spread." The term "spread" in the context of options refers to when there are options with different characteristics, e.g., different strike prices or different expiry dates. In this case, the spread consists of the trader buying the put options while at the same time selling the exact same number of puts with an equal expiration date at a lower strike price. Here, the trader has a cap on the maximum profitability he can get from the option—which in this case means a cap on how much of a loss he is insured against—this maximum amount is the difference between both strike prices. Let's look at an example to make it more clear.

This is called a "bear put spread" since it is typically used when the investor is slightly bearish, and the idea is that the asset's price will decline but not too much. Therefore, the trader sets up this spread where, on the one hand, he can benefit from this decline (from the put with the higher strike price), but on the other hand, he can also minimize the amount he needs to lay out for this benefit (by receiving money from selling the put with the lower strike price).

Let's take a look at an example. There's a stock currently trading at $20, and you, the investor, think that its stock price isn't going anywhere in the immediate future. If you use a bear put spread, you buy a single put option with a $25 strike price for, say, $300 (that would be $3.00 x 100 shares) and simultaneously sell a single put option that has a $20 strike price for $150 (that would be $1.50 x 100 shares). At this point, you would be paying $150 for this spread to be set up (you paid $300 for the put option with a $25 strike price and sold a put option for $150, which equals a total debit of

$150). Suppose the underlying security price closes at $20 or below at expiry. You would make a profit of $350. This is because you make an initial profit of $500 from the options —the difference between the strike prices (($25-$20) x 100 = $500)—this is because although you need to buy the shares at $20 each to honor the put you sold, in turn, you can sell them for $25 each with the right of the put you purchased— a difference of $500. From this initial profit of $500, you have to subtract what you paid for the contracts initially to set up this spread (i.e., the bear put spread). In our case, this is $300-$150, which equals $150. So, in summary, you make $500-$150, which equals $350 profit.

This is how to place a bear put spread when you are slightly bearish; however, for our purposes, we can adapt this idea to use it to hedge when the investor is ultimately not bearish. The benefit of hedging in this way is that you will make the protection put cheaper by making some money back through selling another put at a lower strike price. Let's adapt the case to such a scenario. You hold 100 shares of a stock currently trading at $25, and you believe it can continue to increase in price, yet you want to purchase some protection. If you use a bear put spread, you will buy a single put option with a $25 strike price for, say, $150 (that would be $1.50 x 100 shares) and simultaneously sell a single put option that has a strike price of $20 for $75 (that would be $0.75 x 100 shares). At this point, you would be paying $75 for this spread set-up (you paid $150 for the put option with a $25 strike price and sold a second put option for $75, which equals a total debit of $75). If the price of the underlying security is $20 or below by expiration, you will get a profit of $425. This is because you make an initial profit of $500-the difference between the strike prices (($25-$20) x 100 = $500)-since you need to buy the stock at $20 to honor the put you sold, but in turn, you can sell it for $25 with the rights of the put you purchased. From this initial profit of $500, you have to subtract what you initially paid for the contracts to set up this spread (i.e., the bear put spread). In our case, this was $150-$75, which equals $75. So, $500 minus $75 equals $425, which is our case's total profit from the spread.

Let's have a look at both the pros and cons of this strategy. The obvious advantage is that you can reduce the cost of the protection. Since you are also selling a put, which gives you money, the overall price is cheaper. The disadvantage to this strategy is that you are capping how much protection you have. Since, in our case, any loss up to $20 is covered by the first put (with the higher strike price that you bought), if the position loses even more value and falls below $20, none of it is covered since whatever gain there was from the first put (with the $25 strike price) it is lost by the second put (with the $20 strike price that you sold).

It is also essential to take into account that although he is covered for a five-dollar loss in our case, he also paid another $0.75 for this cover, which needs to be taken into account when calculating gains, losses, and risk potential.

Ultimately, the investor has paid just $0.75 to cover any loss up to $5. This is definitely a strategy to consider since most investors are not looking to hedge against major and sudden collapses since these scenarios are rare and unpredictable. Instead, they are trying to hedge against moderate losses. In this case, the investor has managed to do so for a low price.

Another way of bringing down the cost of protection when hedging with puts is to purchase puts with a longer expiration date. Due to the length of their time value, they are the most expensive to buy as a one-time payment; however, they usually work out as cheaper per day. This means that buying an option with a six-month expiration won't cost double what a three-month expiration would. For example, a three-month option might cost $10, while a six-month option will cost $15. This translates to the six-month option being a whole lot cheaper per day at only $0.08 per day, while the three-month option totals $0.11 a day. There is, in fact, an options contract called a LEAPS option, which is unique in that its expiry dates are far in the future. They are discussed in the next chapter but can be very useful when using long-term contracts for hedging.

Rolling Options

You can optimize this strategy (of using long-term options) by adding a separate strategy known as "rolling options." Let's first discuss rolling options and then come back to hedging. Rolling options is a method used when you move from one call or put option on a specific underlying asset to another call or put option on the same underlying asset. It involves buying a new call or put at the same time as closing your old one. For example, if you own March 130 calls for Microsoft (MSFT), to roll the option, you could sell (to close) the calls that you have and immediately buy (to open) July 130 calls for Microsoft. With most brokers, you can apply this strategy in one transaction, saving you buying and selling commissions. The main goal of the rolling strategy is to make any adjustments to a position that you already have. So, in the above case, you are simply adjusting the expiry date and keeping this position open past the original March expiry date.

An investor would roll his options mainly to lock in profits or manage his time value and theta. Locking in gains happens if, let's say, the investor bought a March 130 call for Microsoft (MSFT) for $2, and it is now worth $6. He can sell the March 130 calls and buy the March 135 calls. He will get $6 for the calls he is closing out and only need to pay $2.50 for the same number of options as the 135 calls (since they are less in the money). This way, he has locked in a $3.50 profit and still has the same exposure to further price increases. The technical term for this is "rolling up" since you are rolling the option to another one with a higher strike price. Similarly, you can roll down an option by buying an option with a lower strike price. Again, you might do this to lock in a profit with puts that you still consider bullish.

Not only can you lock in profits, but you can also use this strategy to extend the life of your options. Using the example above, you owned the March 130 calls of Microsoft and bought the July 130 ones. This effectively extended your position for four months. When you do this, you are mitigating the risk of time decay. As we have discussed, as an option contract nears expiration, it starts to lose its time value at an increasing rate (this is what the theta measures).

Rolling your options well in advance takes away this risk because it means you are never holding the options at their most vulnerable times, which is near their expiration. This type of rolling is called "rolling forward" and is a fundamental strategy when necessary since there is no excuse to hold options with a high theta when you can have the same position with a lower theta. You will also want to utilize rolling forward options when you're confident that the underlying stock will continue to increase. Going back to using puts as a hedge in a cost-efficient way, this strategy of "rolling forward" becomes very important.

As said before, buying options with distant expiry dates already makes a put much cheaper on a per-day basis. What one can now do is buy a put option with an expiry date of 12 months away and, after six months, roll it forward into another 12-month options contract. This roll forward will cost little since there are still six months left until expiry in the option you are selling, so it wouldn't have lost much time value. Therefore, buying the new 12-month contract won't cost much more than the amount received from the sale. One can also roll up or down these options per the price movement of the last six months. Ultimately, an investor can do this every six months; indeed, this is how many investors maintain a hedge on a position for years.

To recap what we have discussed in this chapter, there are many ways you can use options to get the most out of your trades. By incorporating index and ETF options into your portfolio, you can increase exposure and diversification while dealing with less volatility.

We have reviewed the differences between index and ETF options and highlighted the characteristics to consider.

Finally, we also discussed using options as a hedge and the importance of keeping the price paid for them down, along with some practical ways to indeed make this protection cheaper.

In the next chapter, we will talk about techniques and strategies that are more advanced, and that can be very profitable for investors.

8

ADVANCED STRATEGIES

We are now entering the last chapter of the book. If you've read everything until here, you should have a solid foundation of options in general, how they work, what indicators tell you, and some information about basic techniques (it's vital that you go through sections where your knowledge might still be a little shaky to consolidate what we've learned).

This chapter will go through some advanced techniques and strategies you can use when trading options. These present some of the greatest strategies for making profits and are indeed used by all professional and institutional investors. Some of them you might have already heard about; others might be entirely new to you, but rest assured, everything is built on the concepts that you will already be familiar with from this book.

This section of the book might be considered the book's conclusion in that it draws together all the concepts discussed earlier. These methods utilize all option features, such as the Theta and Vega, to earn money in all market circumstances. These methods separate the typical options trader who does not go the extra mile from the option trader who goes the extra mile to advance a level. Indeed, these are the techniques most commonly employed by large institutions.

NEUTRAL STRATEGIES

When we say a strategy is neutral, we are saying it does not have a bullish or bearish bias and is thus unbiased as to which way the market will go. It is important to note that this does not imply that it assumes no price movement at all but rather that it does not presuppose the direction of the movement.

Straddle

The straddle is a neutral strategy. Straddles are utilized when an investor anticipates a high level of volatility in the market but is unsure which way it will move the stock price.

A straddle is when you buy both a call and a put for the same underlying asset with the same expiration date and strike price. With this approach, you benefit when the underlying asset's price rises or falls by more than the combined amount you paid for both premiums. When you anticipate volatility and a large trading range, however, you don't know the direction the move will take, the straddle approach can ensure profits.

Let's look at a hypothetical example to get a clearer idea of the straddle and better understand its use. Let's assume a particular stock has its earnings report released on June 1st, and its current price is $45. You believe the stock price will be volatile after the report's release, but you don't know which direction it will go. (This is a very common example since many volatile stocks experience big swings after their earnings reports if, for example, the company beats earnings estimates or, conversely, misses. Other events can also cause big moves, such as Fed announcements and election results) You would purchase a put and a call at a strike price of $45 (ATM strike prices) with a two-week expiration date (June 15th). To calculate the cost, you then add the premium of the June 15th 45 put and the premium of the June 15th 45 call. In this case, both the put and the call were trading at $1.50 each, so the price of two contracts together is $3.00 (note that we are using only the price of one call contract and one put contract without the 100 multiplier).

Once you have this number, you can figure out how much the underlying price of the asset needs to fall or rise to make a profit. It needs either increase to more than $48 or decrease to more than $42. To work out this number as a percentage, you divide the premium you've paid for both the call and the put ($3.00) by the strike price ($45). In this case, it equals 0.066, which translates to 6.6%. So if the underlying asset's price rises or falls by more than 6.6%, you make a profit.

As with all options trades, there is an opposite position one can take: selling or writing the options as opposed to buying them. In this case, such a position is called a "short straddle," whereas the strategy we described above is technically called a "long straddle" (remember that the word "long" is always used to describe the person holding the asset/s—in this case, options contracts—whereas the term "short" is used for the person selling the asset/s). The investor with a short straddle position is betting on there being low volatility on the underlying stock. Once again, though, there's a big difference in their respective profit and loss profiles. With long straddles, there is no limit on how much you can profit. The profit will be the amount the stock price moves in either direction past the strike price plus the premium. In the above case, anything above $48 or below $42. The maximum loss is the total premium ($3). With a short straddle strategy, your maximum profit is the total premium received, while your loss can be infinite.

This is because when placing a short straddle position, you are selling a call and a put at the same strike price and expiration date instead of purchasing a call and a put at the same strike price and expiration (a long straddle).

The breakeven point for the long and short straddle will be when the stock price has passed the strike price by the amount equal to the premium paid; in this case, this is $42 or $48.

Because the position is supposed to be price neutral, the deltas of all the positions together should come out to be 0 (or very close to 0). This is because the deltas tell us the probability of the asset being in-the-money or out-the-money, and when positioning a straddle, the investor is taking no sides.

Straddles (long) are a solid way of generating significant gains in short periods of time because they can be used when one can predict a big move, such as by an earnings report or other catalyst, as explained above. Of course, long straddles come with their challenges too. The first and most obvious is that you have to be right about the volatility in that it will be more than the market expects. If the underlying stock's price doesn't react as strongly as you have predicted, the stock price will not move past the cost of the premium in either direction (in this case, the maximum loss would be the premium you've paid). But secondly, as significant market events approach, the implied volatility increases, and by extension, so do the prices of both calls and puts, making this strategy relatively expensive. The increase in the price of these options because of the impending event makes it harder for investors to profit from this strategy. This problem can make things worse if, in the end, the expected event does not generate much volatility since this will lead to the extrinsic value of the options evaporating very quickly as the IV value tanks, leaving little value in the options to be salvaged.

This is why you must perform good research. You will want to try and find stocks that have historically had bigger-than-expected moves after their earnings reports. You will also want to look for options with expiration dates where the theta (time decay) is as small as possible and has the smallest effect on the price.

When performing long straddle strategies, you can make money without needing to be right about which way the stock price will go. As we've seen so far with basic options strategies, there's constant pressure to choose between a purchase or a sale and to be right about the price direction. With a long straddle strategy, you can let the market decide this, and this is why straddles are popular.

Strangle

A strangle strategy is in many ways similar to a straddle strategy. The difference is that a strangle strategy uses the same options but at different strike prices. So an investor would have both a call and a put option on the same underlying security with the same expiration date but different strike prices. Similar to the straddle, you can also use the strangle strategy if you think the underlying asset will have significant price movement but don't know in which direction it will move. You only profit if the underlying asset has a significant price move.

You purchase both an OTM call and an OTM put, where the strike price of the call is higher than the value of the asset's current market price, and the put's strike price is lower than its current market price. Again, if the value of the underlying asset rises, you can profit from the call option, and if it decreases, you can profit from the put option. Like with the straddle strategy, you need the asset price to move past any of the strike prices by at least the amount you paid (i.e., both premiums added together) to start making a profit.

Consider the following example. Assume a certain stock is trading at $40 per share. You may use the strangle method by purchasing a call option with a strike price of $42 and a premium of $2.50 for a total cost of $250 (because $2.50 x 100 = $250) and then buying a put option with a strike price of $38 and a premium of $2.35 for a total cost of $235. If the asset's underlying price does not move above or below $38 and $42, you will lose the $485 premium you paid for both options.

But if instead of remaining between $38 and $42 until the expiration date, the stock falls to $28, your call option will expire worthless (and you've lost the $250 you paid for the premium); however, your put option has increased in value and is expiring at $1,000 ($10 of intrinsic value times 100 = $1000). Therefore, overall, you get a profit of $515, the $1000 from your put option, minus the $250 paid for the call, and minus another $235 paid for the put.

It can also happen that the price will move enough for you to get some money back from one of the options, but overall it won't move enough to make an overall profit. Again the breakeven points will be at the call strike price pluss the entire premium or by the put strike price minus the entire premium.

The strangle and straddle strategies differ in that the strangle strategy purchases OTM options while the long straddle approach purchases ATM options. This means that the strangle will have a higher risk and a higher possible profit. Because your strike prices are both OTM in the strangle, there is a much higher probability of both options expiring worthless, which means the underlying asset must move more to generate a profit. On the other hand, the advantages of this technique are that it is less expensive (since OTM options are cheaper) and may therefore provide a considerably larger return if you are correct and the asset price increases significantly above the strike price. The conclusion to be drawn from this is that one should use a strangle when they are more sure about there being a lot of volatility.

Like with the straddle strategy, where one can also take a short straddle position, with the strangle strategy, one can also take a short strangle position by selling the OTM call, and OTM put, with the opinion that there will not be much volatility generated. With this strategy, your profit is limited to the amount you receive for the premium, whereas your risk is unlimited since the asset can rise indefinitely.

Once again, this is a great strategy to take advantage of when you believe there will be a big move, whether from an earnings report, a Fed announcement, or an election result. One should remember when it comes to the long strangle strategy that the further apart the two strike prices are, the higher the risk (and the potential for higher reward).

Covered Calls

Covered calls are a very common strategy in the investing world, and they are also very easy to implement, making them beginner-friendly. It refers to when an investor sells (or writes) call options on a security he already holds. We have spoken before about the dangers of writing calls in that their risk potential is infinite. For example, suppose the option strike price is $20. In that case, the price of the underlying security can keep rising with no limit, so should the stock price end up hitting $100, the writer will have to shell out this $100 to buy the stock in order to then sell it to the purchaser of the option for only $20. With covered calls, however, since the writer owns the underlying security, the writer doesn't have to worry about potentially not having enough money to buy the shares he needs in order to honor the contract he sold. This is why the technique is known as a "covered call," since if the call buyer decides to exercise their options, the writer is protected because they own the underlying stock (and can hence deliver them).

There are good reasons to write covered calls. Once again, this is a neutral strategy for when the investor thinks the stocks he owns will not rise or fall any time soon. In contrast to straddles and strangles, where the investor believes that the stock price will move, he just doesn't know which way; in this case, the investor believes that the price won't move at all.

Over the long term, the investor thinks their position has potential, but they feel that in the meantime, their shares are going to remain relatively flat. Covered calls are one way of using this otherwise "dead" stock to generate income in the interim. If the shares are at $100 and the investor believes that in the next two months, the price will not hit $110, they would then write a $110 call for two months away and sell it for $2. Ultimately, they expect the stock price never to hit the strike price and the option to expire, therefore worthless, meaning they can bag the premium and not have to sell their shares. Should they be correct, this $2 represents a 12% annual return (2% times 6 (2-month periods) = 12%).

One can see why the idea of selling covered calls is so attractive. It provides the investor with a very respectable income from stocks that would otherwise be doing nothing. Indeed, all institutions utilize the idea of covered calls in their portfolios.

The risk of this strategy is that if you are wrong and the price indeed has a big swing, you will lose those extra gains. If the stock price rises well above the strike price, you could end up losing more than you are gaining since you would have to sell the option at the strike price and forfeit the extra value the stock has at the current market value, which may be more than the premium you received. In our example, if the stock price moves to $112, you would have to sell the shares at $110, losing the extra $2. Altogether, you wouldn't lose since you gained $2 from selling the contract, and therefore $112 would be your breakeven point (excluding any commissions paid). However, once the price goes above $112, this means you would have had a bigger profit not writing the call at all. So if the shares hit $120, you would have lost a potential gain of $8 ($120-$112=$8). With covered calls, the loss is a loss of potential gain, not an actual loss, since your shares haven't gone down in value; it is just that you could have made even more should you not have made this move. It is, therefore, smart, as an added part of risk management, to choose a strike price that you would be happy to sell at if it were reached in the short term. So in our example, the investor would choose the $110 strike price because he has already decided that he is happy with a 10% gain in two months on this stock. Therefore even if he ends up being forced to sell at $110, he is happy to take the 10% gain in two months.

This is why this strategy is considered neutral; if the investor is bullish on the stock, he would be better off simply holding the stock rather than taking the risk of selling a call option. In the same way, if he is bearish on the stock, he'd want to sell it since any gains made from the premium would not be enough to cover his loss if the stock price decreased sharply.

When possible, using a tax-deferred account like an IRA is beneficial when performing covered calls. This is because when the trade goes against you and you need to sell your shares, this will trigger a capital gains event that you'd need to report (and pay taxes on). If, however, you use an IRA, for instance, you could sell the shares and then also repurchase them and not have to pay taxes on them.

Butterfly Spread

The butterfly strategy is neutral, and there are two types: the long butterfly and the short butterfly. The first is used when you don't expect movement in either direction, and the latter is mainly used when you do anticipate some movement in either direction. This strategy uses a combination of bear and bull spreads, allowing for limited risk and gains. To use this strategy, you use either a combination of four calls (long call butterfly) or a combination of four puts (long put butterfly) with three different strikes.

To make a long butterfly call, you buy an ITM call with a low strike, sell two ATM calls at the stock price, and buy one OTM call with a high strike. The ITM call and the OTM call are equal distance from the short calls' strike prices (also known as the center strikes). Your maximum profit is reached if the underlying asset's value at the expiration date is equal to the sold calls. The maximum loss happens when the stock price rises above the top strike price or drops below the bottom strike price. This loss is capped at the amount you've paid for the premiums.

Let's look at an example of a long-call butterfly spread in action. A stock is trading at $100, and you believe the price will not fluctuate much in the next few months, so you want to employ this strategy to profit. You sell two $100 calls and buy two more $100 calls, one with a strike price of $95 and the other with a strike price of $105. The cost of the 100 calls you sold was $3.30 per call, for a total profit of $6.60. The 95 calls you purchased cost $6.40, and the 105 calls you purchased cost an additional $1.45. This implies you paid $1.25 total to set up this position. If indeed, at expiration, the stock price is $100, this means that the three options with the higher strike prices all expire worthless, whereas the 95 call expires with $5 of intrinsic value. This will mean that you will have a profit of $5 minus the set-up cost of $1.25, for a total of $3.75. This represents your maximum profit, which can then be said to be the difference between the stock price and the lower strike price, which in this case ($100-$95) is $5 minus the cost of the spread, which in this case was $1.25. Bear in mind that you always need to consider that there are also costs for commissions that need to be subtracted from the total profit. For simplicity's sake, we haven't mentioned it after initially pointing it out. However, it is worth pointing this out again here because buying four options can end with significant amounts paid in commissions. If the stock price ends at $95 or lower, then all the options will expire worthless. This will mean that you have lost nothing from the options, and your total loss will be what you paid for the premiums ($1.25) and commissions.

If the price reaches $105 or above, you will also have lost this amount, but the mechanics will work differently. If the price is exactly $105 at expiration, then the 95 call you purchased will be worth $10. The two 100 call options you sold will both be $5 each in the money, representing a total loss of $10 and canceling out the $10 profit of the 95 call. If these were the only options you had, then every dollar price increase above $105 would be another $1 total loss. This is because you would be getting a $1 profit from the 95 call option you bought, and you would also be incurring a $1 loss from each of the 100 call options you sold, which in this case would total a $2 loss since you sold two options, adding to a total loss of $1. This is why you buy the second call at $105 (called a wing of the butterfly) so that if the stock price keeps going up, you are now also making $2 for every $1 price increase ($1 from the 95 call and $1 from the $105). This cancels out the $2 loss from every $1 increase caused by the 100 call options you sold. Therefore once again, you cap your losses to the net premium of $1.25. Thus, the maximum loss happens when the stock price hits either the lower strike price or the higher strike price, and it is capped at the price of the premium (and commissions).

To understand the breakeven points, it is once again important to understand the mechanics of what is going on in terms of where the gain is coming from and where the losses are coming from, because they are not the same in all cases. When the trade works out, and the stock price is equal to the center strike at expiration, the profit comes from the option with the low strike price that is in the money (in our case, the 95 call). Therefore, when the loss comes from a falling stock price, this will be because as the price starts to fall, the profit begins to evaporate from this in-the-money 95 call as it starts losing its intrinsic value. So in our case, when the stock price is $100, the option has $5 of intrinsic value, but if it falls to $97.50, it has now lost $2.50 of that intrinsic value. All the other options, however, remain worthless. When the positions begin to lose money as the price rises above $100, it is not because the 95 call is losing value; on the contrary, it is gaining value; instead, it is because the sold 100 calls cause you to lose money. So, in this case, if the stock price goes from $100 to $102, the 95 call would now have an extra $2 of value (for a total of $7); however, the two 100 calls that were sold will have also created a loss of $2 each, canceling out the $2 gain of the 95 call and adding another $2 loss, thereby creating a net loss of $1 for every $1 the price rises (until $105, where the 105 call cancels out this loss as explained above).

Now that we understand this let's look at the breakeven points. If the stock price goes down, then he will only start to have a loss once the 95 call isn't making enough to cover the net premium, meaning the breakeven point for when the stock price goes down is the bottom strike plus the premium paid. In our case, this is $95 plus $1.25, which is $96.25, since at this point the 95 option is $1.25 in the money, which is the same amount you lost through paying the set-up premium. When the price goes above $100, then the breakeven point is the upper strike price minus the net premium since, at this point, there is only $1.25 of value remaining from the 95 call, which hasn't yet been canceled out by the two 100 calls sold.

As previously stated, the purpose of this technique is to profit from a stock that does not move. We've seen that there are additional strategies to profit from equities that don't move, such as short straddles and short strangles (where you sell the OTM call and the OTM put, which is the opposite of a long strangle and long straddle). These methods will also earn you more money than the butterfly spread (since you are not buying any options, only selling). However, the main advantage of the butterfly spread is that you have reduced your possible loss by purchasing the wings (the 95 and 105 calls).

Once we understand this, we can easily adjust it also to understand the long put butterfly spread since it works the same way as the long call butterfly spread and has the same maximum profit, maximum loss, and breakeven points. It is done by purchasing an OTM put option with a low strike, writing two ATM puts, and buying an ITM put with a high strike price. The maximum profit is reached if the underlying price is at the center strike by expiration, and the position starts to lose value if the price moves in either direction until no option value is left. The maximum loss is the net premium paid, just like with a long call butterfly. The only thing you need to do is change the direction of where the money is being made, so when the price does indeed not move and stays at $100, the profit is coming from the option with the higher strike price (of $105) and not from the one with the lower strike price (of $95). This is because with puts the higher strike price is always more in-the-money, and with calls, it is always the lower strike price that is more in-the-money.

As with all option strategies, one can also short the butterfly by taking the opposite side of these positions. This will also give you the opposite maximum gain and maximum loss points. This entails writing the options you need to buy to be long and buying the options you need to write to be long. In these cases, you are betting on the price moving as opposed to staying flat. Your maximum profit is the net premium received, and your maximum loss is the difference between a strike price at the wing and the center strikes ($5) minus the premium you received.

The most common form of the butterfly is actually another type of butterfly spread called an iron butterfly. It also seeks to take advantage of little price movement and decreasing volatility. It, too, is a four-option combination, but this time it consists of two calls and two puts. Here you can sell (write) two ATM options, one call and one put. Then you buy an OTM call at a higher strike, and an OTM put at a lower strike price. You can look at this as a short straddle (i.e., the two at-the-money options you are selling) while buying an OTM call for upside protection and another OTM put for downside protection. This means that you are trying to make money in the form of receiving premiums from the sold options while giving away a bit of the profit to buy OTM options for protection. Since this is the case, this is why you are selling ATM options (which are expensive) while only buying OTM options (which are cheaper). This means an iron butterfly is a net credit spread (i.e., you end with a credit after creating the position) where your aim is to keep as much money as possible. Once again, there are other strategies one can use, such as a simple short straddle, but here the wings (i.e., the OTM options) limit the amount you can lose.

Let's break this down with an example. Assume a stock has just had a quick, solid move to $40 because it released good data, and you believe that it has now priced in all the good news, and its rally should slow down and the price settle around here. You can now write a $40 put and a 40 call for $5 each, for a total of $10, since the high volatility is making the options expensive. This is the money you want to keep as much of as possible. Then you buy a 35 put for $2.00 and a 45 call for $5.50 for a total purchase price of $7.50. This is money you intend to lose since you are buying these options as protection in case of a worst-case scenario. In this example, your net credit from the spread is $2.50. If this trade plays out according to plan, and indeed, by expiry, the price is at $40, this will mean that all options expire worthless, and you walk away with the maximum profit, which is your net credit from the spread. Once again, it is worth pointing out that the maximum profit is actually the net credit minus what you spend on commissions since you need to pay attention to commissions as they can add up when trading many options. Although this is the maximum profit, it may be worth closing out the trades early if the prices of the options tank very quickly. For example, let's say the high volatility suddenly drops, and all the options are half the price within a couple of days. If this is the case, it may be worth buying back the written options with a "buy to close" order (for $5 altogether, since they are now half price) and selling the bought options with a "sell to close" order (for $3.75 altogether). This way, you already have a significant profit in a short period of time ($1.25, since you paid $1.25 to close the order and got $2.50 when you opened it) and don't need to run the risk of the price moving over the long period left, or the risk of the contracts getting assigned. Suppose the trade goes against you, and the stock price moves. If it increases to exactly $45 per share, in that case, the call you sold will now represent a $5 loss because the investor who bought it can demand he buys it from you for only $40, and all other options expire worthless, leaving you with this loss of $5 minus the $2.50 net credit you received from the premiums, resulting in a $2.50 loss. If the price goes from $45 to $47, your loss will still be the same since the extra $2 you lose from the 40 call you sold is canceled out by the 45 call you bought, which is now worth $2. This means the most you can lose from an upward movement in price is the difference between the center strike price ($40) and the upper strike price ($45) minus the net credit received.

When the price goes down, it will also have the same consequences since, as the mirror image of the price going up, if the price goes down to $35, there is a $5 loss on the 40 put that was sold, and all the other options expire worthless, so there will be a $5 loss minus the net credit, which is $2.50. If the price continues to fall to $33, the loss will remain the same because, while the 40 put now has another $2 loss for a total loss of $7, the 35 put that you purchased will offset that loss with a $2 gain. This means we can expand the above rule so that the maximum loss (in whichever direction) will be the difference between one of the strikes at the wings (45$ or $35) and the center strikes ($40) minus the net credit received. The breakeven will be the center strike (the ATM 40 call and put) plus or minus the credit received (in this case, $42.50 and $37.50).

For the sake of comprehensiveness, we should mention that, while less common, there is also an opposing side to the trade. This is for when you anticipate that the price will go to the extremes of this range, and you set it up by reversing the option types. Therefore, you write the OTM options rather than purchasing them, and you purchase the ATM options rather than writing them. This will be a net debit spread (meaning you will have a net debit once you have finished creating the position), giving you the most profit if the stock price reaches the outer strike prices and your maximum loss is equal to the net debit for the premium.

Condor Spread

The condor spread is another neutral strategy that allows the investor to profit from high or low volatility while limiting both losses and gains. The condor spread is like the butterfly spread in many ways. The strategic difference between them is that when you perform a condor strategy, you are expanding the trade's area of profit and, on the other hand, limiting its profit potential. Like the butterfly, you have long and short condors. The long is when you want to set a strategy to profit from low volatility (or no movement) in the underlying stock, while the short condor allows you to profit from high volatility in the underlying asset's price in any direction.

One of the characteristics of this strategy is that it mitigates risks. This ultimately also restricts profits and adds to the set-up costs since you need several options. Like the butterfly spread, you use four options, either all puts or all calls with the same expiry date. The difference between the butterfly set-up and the condor set-up is you have four strike prices in a condor, whereas with a butterfly, you only have three.

As with the butterfly spread, we will focus on the long condor spread, which is when you don't expect price movement. A long call condor uses two strategies we mention below: a bull call spread and a bear call spread. As mentioned, a condor spread has four strike prices rather than three. The distances of these calls will mirror each other, so you sell (write) two calls at an equal distance from the current stock price and then buy two calls at an equal distance from the calls you sold.

Let's look at an example of a long condor spread with calls. Once again, your aim is to profit from low volatility since you believe the stock price won't move. In the case of the condor, the stock can be anywhere between the two middle strikes at expiration to reach maximum profit. If you have a stock trading at $45, you might sell (write) two calls, one a 40 call for $7 and the second a 50 call for $2. This means you receive a total of $9 for this leg of the position. At the same time, you purchase two calls, the first being a 35 call for $11.50 and the second a 55 call for $0.50. This means you pay $12 for the second leg of the position.

All in all, this position has cost you a debit of $3 ($12-$9), or $300, once multiplied by 100 for the number of underlying shares in a contract. Let's first look at a case where the trade works out. If at expiration, the stock price is anywhere between $40 and $50, this will mean the two calls with the highest strike prices (i.e., the 50 call and the 55 call) will expire worthless, whereas the combination of the other two options will give you a $5 profit. This is because, at the price of $40, the 35 call is at a profit of $5, and any extra profit this call will get from the price being above $40 until $50 will be canceled out by the 40 call that was written. So if, for example, the stock price is $42, the additional $2 profit the 35 call now has is canceled by the sold 40 call, which represents a $2 loss. Now that we have an options gain of $5, we have to subtract from the overall profit the price it cost to make this position, which was $3, meaning the biggest possible gain is $2 ($5-$3). Therefore, the maximum gain is the difference between the lowest and second lowest strike prices minus the net debit used to make the position (and minus the commissions, as already discussed in the section on butterfly spreads). This illustration explains why the condor has a wider area for maximum gain than a butterfly; the maximum profit is reached in a $10 range (between $40 and $50). However, the gain of $2 at its peak is relatively modest compared to the maximum possible loss described later.

Let's now consider what happens when the price doesn't stay in the preferred range. If it leaves this range through a price decrease, then when it hits $35 or lower, all the options will expire worthless, resulting in a loss of the premium paid, which, as said, is a net debit of $3. In the area between $35 and $40, the gain and loss fluctuate depending on the price. However, we can calculate that the bottom strike price of $35 plus the $3 premium, which is $38, gets us to the breakeven point where there is no loss or gain. If the price leaves the predicted range through a price increase, the calculations are the same, but the mechanics are different. If the price hits $55, then again, there is no profit from the options, and the total loss will be the loss of the net debit for the premiums.

The reason is that although the gain from the 35 call option is $20, its practical gain will never be more than $5 because once the stock price hits $40, the position starts to lose money from the sold 40 call option, and this loss will cancel any additional gains from the 35 call. To sum up, the two options with the lowest strike prices result in a $5 gain, however high the price goes. The next option, which is the 50 call that was also sold, will start to create a loss as the price rises above $50. Once it reaches $55, it now represents a $5 loss, which cancels out the $5 gain that the position had from the first two options. This is why when the stock price reaches $55, there is no gain or loss from the options, and the total result is just the loss of the total premium paid. Once the stock price keeps going above $55, any extra loss that the 50 call will cause is canceled out by the 55 call that was bought and now starts to gain. So if the price hits $57, although the 50 call now represents a loss of $7, the 55 call has a gain of $2, and therefore there is still just a $5 loss from the two options with the highest strike prices. It can thus be summarized that when the price goes up, the maximum loss is the debit paid for the premiums and that a breakeven price can be calculated as the top strike price minus the premium, which in this case is $52.

With this understanding, it will be simple to comprehend a long condor with puts. The biggest gain will be when the price stays within the range of the two middle puts, and the maximum loss will be when the price approaches the wings. The difference is in the mechanics of the direction of value, in that when the stock price is at $55, all the options expire worthless (as opposed to the long call condor, where the options expire worthless when the price is at $35), and when the stock price is at $35, the (highest three) puts have value but cancel each other out (as the calls do when the stock price is at $55). This is because the puts with the highest strike prices have the most intrinsic value.

As with the butterfly, the short variant (technically known as the short condor) may also be set up with calls or puts. It is the inverse of a long condor in that the person who takes such a position is betting for movement up to the spread's wings. You purchase the calls (or puts) that you would write if you were executing the long condor and sell the calls you would buy if you were doing the long condor. The maximum profit is also the opposite and is the premium received ($3) since this is now a net credit spread. The maximum loss is the difference between the outer and inner strike prices minus the net credit received for the spread.

The short version of the condor and the butterfly are not very used strategies since one can create a position that also benefits from volatility where there is no cap to how much the gain can be, such as the straddle and strangle. This is in contrast to the long condor (and butterfly), where other strategies that benefit from no movement (such as short straddles and strangles) in the underlying's price don't offer the same protection that one gets from a condor or butterfly (where the losses are limited). Therefore a beginner should start with the long version of these strategies, and then, if he finds that the short version has a place in his overall strategy, he can incorporate it.

As with the butterflies, the most common type of condor is the iron condor. An iron condor involves two puts (one short and one long) and two calls (one short and one long) with four different strike prices but the same expiration date. In this strategy, too, the objective is to try and profit from the low volatility of the stock. The payoff structure here is identical to the normal condor spread in terms of attaining maximum profit when the stock price expires between the middle strike prices and a maximum loss when the stock price hits one of the outer strike prices (i.e., the wings). The difference between the two payoff structures is where the profit comes from; with the iron condor, the profit is made by keeping the premiums received since it is a net credit strategy, whereas, with the long condor, the gain comes from having an in-the-money option. To build this method, you need to purchase one OTM put with a strike price below the price of the stock; and sell (write) another OTM put with a closer strike price to the stock's current price; then you need to sell (write) one slightly OTM call option above the stock's current price and purchase another OTM call with a strike price further out than the one you sold. The two inner options that are sold should be at an equal distance from the stock price, and similarly, the two outer strike prices (which are bought) should be at an equal distance from the stock price and the other options. This will mean you end with a net credit since the options sold are nearer to being in the money and hence more expensive than the options you are buying. As with the iron butterfly, the maximum profit is the net credit (or total premiums) you get from establishing the position. Your maximum loss is limited to the difference between the long (bought) and short (sold) option strike prices minus the net premiums. The breakeven point will be the short (sold) option's strike price plus the net premium when the stock price increases and minus the net premium when the stock price decreases.

These neutral strategies (the straddle, strangle, butterfly, and condor) have been explained in a completely neutral way with equidistant strike prices and neutral deltas. However, one can also play around and change these numbers if he has a bias towards one side more than the other, for example, if he uses an iron condor thinking that there won't be movement but believes that there is more chance of an increase in price than a price decrease, he can adjust his middle options to give him more room on the upper price side to account for the probability that the price might go that way.

BULLISH STRATEGIES

Married Put

A married put is similar to the protective put stated previously. The difference between a married put and a protective put is that with the protective put, you already own the underlying stock and are simply hedging it. With a married put, you buy both the put option and the underlying stock simultaneously and instruct your broker not to acquire the shares unless the put option is also delivered. A married put is considered a bullish strategy since you buy it while you are bullish on the company and only add the put because you are concerned that the stock's value may fall. Therefore, in a married put, you hold the stock and buy a put option that is near-the-money to serve as protection in case the price of the stock goes down.

The benefit of this strategy is that you can still have an unlimited gain from the stock's appreciation while your potential losses on the stock are capped. In many other strategies where the loss is capped, it often comes with a limit on the amount that can be gained. The downside of this strategy, once again, is that the cost of the premium to purchase the option can be significant. Therefore, it is best to employ the married put when the stock has low volatility, and you are worried about a potential announcement that could negatively affect the stock price, such as an earnings report, a Fed announcement, or election results.

Let's look at an example where the underlying stock actually decreases in value to understand the protection a married put allows. Say you purchase 100 shares of a stock at $30 per share, as well as one put at $27.50 for $0.50 (which means you pay altogether $50 since $0.50 x 100 shares = $50). You now have a regular stock position at $30 per share and protection if there's a decrease in the stock price. Imagine the value of the underlying stock decreased to $25. Technically, you've lost $5 per share on your stock holding, but since you have a put with a strike price of $27.50, which means you can still sell these $25 options at $27.50, it means your loss is only $2.50 (i.e., the difference between $30 and $27.50). This means that you have saved yourself $2.50 in losses.

To completely calculate the risk-reward profile, the premium of $0.50 also needs to be included, meaning that the loss is $3 (excluding any commissions), and only $2 was saved.

This must also be included when calculating your winnings; so, while your position might rise indefinitely, you must subtract the premium from the final amount to determine how much you really gained. In our example, if the stock rises to $32, the gain is $1.50 ($2-$0.50). This means the breakeven mark is $30.50.

It is very easy to work out the floor of your losses. It is always the strike price of the option minus the premium (as well as commissions). If you were to purchase a put with a strike price at the exact current market price, then the floor of your losses is the price of the premium alone.

Essentially, this position acts like a long call option in that its profit potential is limitless, and its risk is capped.

The benefit that the married put gives the investor over the long call (and the reason why he would use this strategy) is that he can hold the stock, giving him the rights that come with that, such as collecting dividends and having voting rights, while still not spending or risking more than the value of a regular premium.

As previously stated, this protection can be quite high, so it is best used if you believe there may be short-term uncertainty in the stock you are holding; or if you are a new investor who wants to start using more advanced strategies and knowing that your losses are limited will give you the confidence you need to begin testing your skills.

Bull Spread

A bull spread is a slightly bullish strategy that allows you to get returns from an increase in the underlying asset's price while limiting potential losses. This technique falls into the category of methods called "vertical spreads," which involve purchasing and selling options of the same type and expiration date but with different strike prices. These techniques are called "vertical" because the difference between the positions lies in the strike prices of each, which is represented as a vertical line. All of the spreads discussed until now have been of this sort; however, some combined more than one vertical spread together.

Within bull spreads, there are two varieties of the strategy: one using two call options appropriately called a bull call spread, and one using two put options called a bull put spread. Regardless of whether it's with calls or puts, in this strategy, you purchase one option with a lower strike price and write another option with a higher strike price.

Because the option you buy in the bull call spread is more expensive than the option you sell (because calls with lower strike prices are more expensive because they are more likely to be in the money), you create a net debit when using this strategy. This is why a bull call spread is also called a debit call spread. With the bull put spread, the option that you buy is cheaper than the option that you sell (since with puts, the higher the strike price, the more expensive the option is since, the higher strike prices are more likely to be in the money), and therefore, when placing this type of spread, you are creating a net credit. Because of this, bull put spreads are also called credit put spreads.

Cash flow and timing are what distinguish these two forms of bull spreads. As previously stated, a bull call spread is also known as a debit call spread since you pay upfront, and your returns will (ideally) arrive later when the underlying moves before the options expire. With a bull put spread, you're collecting profit first and waiting to see and hold on to as much as possible by when the options expire. Because you're receiving a premium for selling an option, your initial investment will always be cheaper when compared to only buying options. Let's look at these two types of bull spreads more closely to see how they play out. Let's say, for instance, that you want to do a bull call spread on the S&P 500, and the S&P 500 is currently trading at $4400, and you can buy a SPX 4400 call for $31.50 and sell a SPX 4405 call for $30. This brings the net debit of the bull call spread to $150 since $31.50-$29 = $1.50 (and when multiplied by 100, it equals $150). If the SPX were at $4405 by expiry, then the 4400 call you purchased would be worth $5, while the 4405 call you sold would have expired worthless. This would mean you have a profit of $5 from the options, minus the premium of $1.50 you paid for the position. This means that, altogether, you made a profit of $3.50.

You can also see that this is the most you can make because even if the SPX rose to $4410, your options profit would still only be $5 since although your 4400 call would be worth $10, this would be offset by the 4405 call that you sold, which would result in a $5 loss (because you need to buy the SPX at $4410 and then sell it at $4405). If the SPX price falls, both options will expire worthless, and the only money you will lose is the total amount spent on the options, which is only $1.50. You have traded some potential gain to get a cheap position.

Let's now see how this plays out as a bull put spread. The SPX is trading at $4400, and you anticipate that the index will increase. So you sell the SPX 4401 put for $32 and buy the 4395 put for $30, leaving you with a $2 profit (for a total of $200 when multiplied by 100). Here you have already received all your potential profits, and the aim is to keep as much as possible. If the index rises above $4401, as you predicted, you can keep your profits. On the other hand, should the index decrease to $4395, the 4401 put you sold represents a $6 loss (since you need to buy the $4395 index for $4401), and the 4395 put you bought expires worthless. This leaves you with an option loss of $6 and a premium gain of $2 for a total loss of $4 (or $400 in total). This represents the biggest possible loss because even if the price continues to drop to, say, $4390, and the 4401 put you sold now represents an $11 loss, this will be offset by the 4395 put that you purchased, which will now be $5 in profit.

To sum up, with both spreads, maximum profit is achieved when the underlying asset's price indeed appreciates. With the bull call spread, the maximum possible profit is the difference between the two options minus the total debit paid for the premiums (ignoring any commissions). The maximum loss is the debit paid for the premiums. The breakeven point, where there is no loss or gain, is the lower strike price plus the total debit paid (again, ignoring any commissions), which in the above example is $4401.50. For the bull put spread, it is the opposite way around. The maximum gain possible is the net credit received from taking this position (again, ignoring commissions). The maximum loss is the difference between the two strike prices minus the net credit received, and the breakeven point is the higher strike price minus the net credit, which in the above bull put case is $4399.

The benefit of using this strategy is that you have exposed yourself to the possible gains while limiting your potential losses. The disadvantage is that you have limited the size of your potential gains. This is why this strategy is for when you are moderately bullish.

The bull spread is a great way to benefit from moderate price increases without putting too much money at risk. It also allows you to enter the position without needing much initial capital, and in the case of the bull put spread, you don't need any capital at all.

Protective Collar

A protective collar is created by using two strategies we have already discussed; the protective put and the covered call.

The idea of the protective collar is to protect a long stock position against a price decline. This means that when we say it is a bullish strategy, we don't mean it in the sense that the investor believes a price increase is about to happen. Instead, we mean it in the sense that it is for an investor who is long on a stock position because he thinks that the price will eventually go up, although he doesn't necessarily believe that it is going up in the immediate future. This strategy is for the investor to protect his position in the meantime.

Before we explain how a protective collar works, let's first talk about what a collar is.

A collar is a method that utilizes two options by having one on either side of the stock price. This is why the name collar is used. It is usually a strategy that protects against large losses, which in turn also limits the gains that are possible to earn.

To understand a protective collar, let's dive in with an example of an investor already long on an underlying stock who wants some extra protection. To perform the protective collar, he would purchase an OTM put option (i.e., with a strike price lower than the market price of the stock) while writing an OTM call option at the same time (i.e., with a strike price above the market price of the stock). The OTM put will protect him if the stock price falls while selling the call will get him cash (i.e., the premium) to cover the cost of buying the put. It will also allow him to still earn a return on the stock if it goes up until the call's strike price. One of the main benefits of the protective collar is that the investor is essentially selling an option to buy another one, which can make the cost of performing this method very cheap. To reiterate, this is not for an investor who thinks that his investment has a lot of potential in the near future; on the contrary, since one sells an OTM call, this call will limit gains from appreciation. This strategy focuses on protecting against stock price declines, not on making profits.

To summarize, to create a protective collar, you need to have a long position on an underlying stock, buy a put option to get protection from the stock price falling, and sell a call option to fund the put.

When you purchase the put and write the call, they are both OTM and have the same expiration date. They create the "collar." Because the goal of the collar is to hedge the risk of the underlying stock's value falling, and the call you sell is to get this protection for as cheap as possible, you will want the sale of the covered call to cancel out the money needed for the premium of the put. This will generally be the case if the strike prices are equal distance from the stock price. For instance, if the stock is trading at $40 and the call strike price is $45, the put should have a strike price of $35.

Aside from protecting your investments at a low cost, the collar strategy can also help you save money on taxes. For instance, if you've held an asset that has increased in price since you bought it, and you believe that it is a solid long-term holding but that in the short term, the market environment will make it too volatile to hold. One of your simplest options is to sell the stock and repurchase it when the market is more stable. The problem with this is that selling will make you liable for capital gains tax on your returns. When you use the collar strategy, you can reduce the risk of loss by hedging instead of selling and, therefore, save yourself from needing to sell, triggering a tax event. If the shares go up and the buyer of the call exercises their options, you'll have to sell and pay taxes on any profit you've made. But assuming you are right and the price doesn't go up, so the call option is never exercised, you will be saving yourself from any tax events.

BEARISH STRATEGIES

Bear Spread

A bear spread is the opposite of a bull spread and is used when the trader is slightly bearish about a stock and wants to profit from this while minimizing his risk. Like in a bull spread, this involves buying and selling two puts or two calls with the same expiration date on the same underlying stock, with different strikes. Like in a bull spread, in a bear spread, you also have two types of strategies: a bear call spread and a bear put spread, with the first being a spread made of calls and the second being a spread made of puts. In contrast with bull spreads, you always buy the option with the higher strike price and sell the option with the lower strike price. This also leads to the bear put and bear call spread payout being the opposite of the bull spread. Since you are buying the option with the higher strike price, in the case of the bear put, it ends up being a net debit (since puts with higher strike prices are more expensive), and with the bear call, the position ends up with a net credit (since the calls with higher strike prices are cheaper). The amount and timing of the payout will be the inverse of the bull call, with the bear call being the net credit and immediate, and the bear put dependent on how far the underlying moves by expiry, as discussed further below. The intuitive difference between bear and bull spreads is that with bear spreads, you reach your maximum profit when the underlying stock closes at or below the lower strike price, whereas with bull spreads, you reach your maximum profit when the underlying stock closes at or above the higher strike price.

Let's look at examples of the two styles, starting with a bear put spread. Imagine you are bearish on a particular stock, and it is trading at $40. You think that within the next month, the price of that stock will go down. Here, you can perform a bear put by purchasing a 38 put and selling a 34 put at a $1 spread cost. In the best-case scenario, you'll see the price at or below $34. When it is at $34, the 38 put option will have made you a profit of $4, and the 34 put option will expire worthless. If the stock price goes even lower, say to $32, the profit stays the same because although the 38 put option is now worth $6, the extra profit is canceled out by the sold 34 put option, which represents a $2 loss. Therefore, in the best-case scenario, the gain is $4 from the options, which, together with the $1 debit you paid for the spread, equals a total gain of $3. In the worst-case scenario, you'll see the price of the underlying stock being at or above $38, where all the options expire worthless and your total loss is the $1 you spent setting up the position. This is the most you can lose. Once again, you lay out money to make the position (debit) and (hopefully) make a profit by the underlying moving in your favor before the expiry. In this case, the maximum gain is the difference between the two strike prices ($38-$34=) $4 minus the debit paid to set up the position ($1), which is $3. The maximum loss is the debit paid, which is $1, and the breakeven point where there is no loss or gain is the higher strike price minus the debit paid, which in this case would be $37 (highest strike minus spread cost, which is $38-$1 = $37).

Let's now look at a bear call spread with the same example. The stock is trading at $40, and you think it will decrease within the next month. You write a 34 call option, purchase a 38 call option, and receive a credit spread of $3. If the underlying stock price is at or below $34, you keep the spread credit of $3 because both options expire worthless. However, you will reach a maximum loss if the underlying stock price is at or above $38. If the stock price is exactly $38, then the 34 call option you sold is now at a $4 loss, and the 38 call option you bought is worthless. Even if the price goes further up and reaches, say, $40, your options loss will still be $4 since, although the 34 call option is now at a $6 loss, this is offset by the 38 call option you bought, which will now be $2 in profit. Either way, your options will have caused you a $4 loss. This, taken together with the $3 net credit you received when creating these positions, means your total loss is $1. You can see that the bear call spread makes its profit at the outset and then (hopefully) retains it until expiry. In this case, the maximum profit is the net credit. The maximum loss is the difference between the strike prices, which is ($38-$34=$4), minus the net credit of

$3 for a total of $1, and the breakeven here is the lower strike price plus the net credit ($34 + $3), which equals $37.

We have now discussed the four types of vertical option spreads. We have a bull call, a bear call, a bull put, and a bear put.

Let's consider some practical scenarios when the different styles are relevant.

For a bull call spread, an example of when you would want to use it is when the market is reaching its peak or at the later stages of a bull market, when volatility is high, and you are only moderately bullish on the stock price's potential.

Conversely, a bear call spread can be used when you believe there will be a mild downturn in the stock and there's also high volatility (in this case, the high volatility benefits you because you can collect a bigger premium). You can find this environment after a correction in the market or in the late stages of a bear market.

A bull put spread is often used when trying to make extra premium income in sideways and slightly downward markets. You can also cleverly use this strategy to buy stocks at a discount, for if the put you wrote gets exercised at the strike price, you are essentially buying it for less than the market price since you received a net credit when you entered the position. You should therefore consider bull puts when you would otherwise buy the dip in a correction of an overall upward trend.

Besides using a bear put spread when you believe the market might go down slightly and there is high volatility, you can also use it to hedge long positions (i.e., positions you hold because you are bullish) in a low volatility environment (where hedges aren't prohibitively expensive anyway) by making the hedge even cheaper through the premium you receive from the put you write. Getting a good grip on bull and bear spreads is very important since many of the neutral strategies (which are the most useful and hence the most popular) are built on bull and bear spreads.

LEAPS

LEAPS, or long-term equity anticipation securities, are options that have a longer expiration date than a normal option (usually more than one year) and are valid for up to three years from the date of issue. They work in the same way other options do, with the difference being that their expiration date is a lot further away. Much like with regular options we've seen so far, LEAPS allow you to have the right, but not the obligation, to buy or sell the underlying stock at a specific price (the strike price) before or on the expiration date. Here, you also pay a premium to acquire the option.

The main difference between a LEAPS contract and a regular options contract is that, due to the length of time before the expiry date, the underlying asset price movements have a smaller effect on the premium. This gives an investor a chance to have an option with lower volatility. The other main benefit of the LEAPS contract also comes from the fact that the expiry is so far out, and that is that they are a very cheap way of hedging because, as explained in the last chapter, the investor can roll them for a relatively low price. There are a couple of disadvantages to LEAPS. One is that they are more expensive to buy as a one-time payment since they have so much time value, even though, as explained earlier, they are significantly cheaper on a per-day basis. Another potential disadvantage is that you are committing your money for a much longer period of time than you are with a short-term option contract.

To reiterate, other than the differences that come from the fact that the expiry is later, there are no differences in the actual mechanics and characteristics of a LEAPS and a standard option contract. They can be called calls or puts, be purchased or written, and are a cheaper way of controlling more stock; they make and lose money the same way.

OTHER CONSIDERATIONS

It's important to pay attention to the indicators we've mentioned in the previous chapters when trading options and using different strategies, such as the IV and the Greeks. You also need to look at the risk-reward ratio, which is defined by the potential reward you can earn for every dollar you spend when investing. You can use risk/reward ratios to compare the expected returns of your investments and the amount of risk you have to take to earn the profits. For instance, if you invest with a risk/reward ratio of 1:5, this tells you that you are risking $1 for the potential earning of $5.

When added to the indicators we've talked about, this will help you analyze what method you should use when considering your overall plan and risk profile. For instance, if you are indecisive between using a butterfly spread or a condor spread, you need to know that a butterfly spread has an overall better risk-reward ratio, but with the condor strategy, you have greater chances of winning a trade (because it has a better delta). On the other hand, the butterfly technique has a better theta return since you are selling ATM options that decay faster and offer you a better chance at a quick trade. In the same way, you will also want to use the delta to understand the probability of winning with different strike prices within your chosen strategies.

WHEN TO SELL?

In this last section, we will look at one of the most critical things in options trading and investments in general: when to exit a trade and take profits.

To profit from options trading, it is obviously essential that you purchase options that will increase in value, but knowing when to exit and take profits is just as important. There are a lot of profit opportunities in options when there's exceptionally high volatility; however, if you miss the right opportunity to exit your position, it can lead to losing a lot of that profit (plus, more often than not, the entire position). Let's go through some of the best exit strategies.

TRAILING STOP

This is a great and often-used profit-taking strategy. With this strategy, you predetermine a percentage below the current price that you will sell. For instance, with stocks as the example, you set a percentage level of 25%. If you have purchased ten shares of a particular stock at $90 per share for a total of $900, and the stock falls to $67.5 a share (a 25% drop), the trailing stop will trigger, and you will sell. If the price first goes up to $135, you adjust your trailing stop to 25% of the new price, which in this case will be $101.25, thereby locking in an $11.25 gain. However, you need to do things slightly differently in the case of options. Since options are so volatile, you can't start with a trailing stop, or you will always get stopped out. Instead, you need first to pick a profit target that you are happy with, and once you hit that point, you then activate (whether manually or through automation) the trailing stop with the percentage you have determined.

This way, you create continuous protection as the options increase in value.

PARTIAL PROFIT BOOKING

A partial profit booking is done by setting up a profit target, at which point you take a portion of the profits. For example, if an option you bought for $1000 has reached a 50% gain (to $1500), you cash out with 50% of the option's entire value ($750). If the value increases another 50% to $1125, you can take another 50% of the option's value off ($562.50). You keep doing this until your option expires, at which point you cash out whatever remaining value is left in whatever way you deem best to close your option, as discussed in Chapter 3. Using this technique will allow you to take gains and protect your capital to a certain extent while still leaving room for further appreciation. One standard version of this used by investors is to take 50% off after a 100% increase, which means they have taken the capital off and are now playing with "the house's" money.

As you can see, there is no simple answer when it comes to volatile options. Before you consider taking anything off the table, you need to set a sensible profit objective, at the very least. The major takeaway should be that as the profits start rolling in, don't let the illogical notion that it will continue to rise until expiry take over, but rather have the discipline to cash in on a portion of your profits.

Options can be highly volatile; on the one hand, this makes for great opportunities to profit; however, without a good exit strategy, these gains will most likely be lost.

CONCLUSION

There's a lot to understand in the world of options. If you're starting out, it's vital that you go through the content of this book thoroughly to understand all the material fully and to refer back when necessary. In this book, we have traveled from the basics of what options are and what they are composed of to the more advanced techniques by the end of the book. Ultimately, having all the necessary knowledge to trade options is only half the work; the other half necessary to becoming a complete options trader is getting your hands dirty. Once you start trading, the knowledge you have gained will come to life through seeing these concepts play out and getting an intuitive feel for what moves and measurements are considered large or small.

By reaching the end of the book, you have demonstrated that you are the sort of person who wants to learn more and accepts responsibility for the outcomes in their life. This means you have the personality to become a successful investor and options trader. Now go and use the information in this book to that end. Have great success!

REFERENCES

Delta Explained: Understanding Options Trading Greeks - Merrill Edge. https://www.merrilledge.com/investment-products/options/learn-understand-delta-options

Option Greeks: The 4 Factors to Measure Risk - Investopedia. https://www.investopedia.com/trading/getting-to-know-the-greeks/

The Top Technical Indicators for Options Trading - Investopedia. https://www.investopedia.com/articles/active-trading/101314/top-technical-indicators-options-trading.asp

Printed in Great Britain
by Amazon

76692095-2e32-4791-a36b-cfecb302d7b9R01